BASIC CONCEPTS

Studies in Continental Thought

Martin Heidegger

BASIC CONCEPTS

Translated by

GARY E. AYLESWORTH

Indiana University Press
Bloomington & Indianapolis

This book is a publication of

Indiana University Press
601 North Morton Street
Bloomington, Indiana 47404-3797 USA

www.indiana.edu/~iupress

Telephone orders   800-842-6796
Fax orders   812-855-7931
Orders by e-mail   iuporder@indiana.edu

Published in German as *Grundbegriffe* © 1981
by Vittorio Klostermann, Frankfurt am Main

English translation © 1993 by Indiana University Press
First paperback edition 1998

Manufactured in the United States of America

Library of Congress Cataloging-in-Publication Data

Heidegger, Martin, 1889–1976.
　　[Grundbegriffe. English]
　　Basic concepts / Martin Heidegger ; translated by Gary E.
Aylesworth.
　　　　p.　　cm. — (Studies in Continental thought)
　　Includes bibliographical references.
　　ISBN 0-253-32767-9 (alk. paper). —
　　ISBN 0-253-21215-4 (pbk. : alk. paper)
　　1. Philosophy, German—20th century.　2. Philosophy, German—Greek
influences.　I. Title.　II. Series.
B3279.H48G7613　1993
193—dc20　　　　　　　　　　　　　　　　　　92-46633

2　3　4　5　6　03　02　01　00　99　98

Contents

Contents

TRANSLATOR'S FOREWORD

The present volume is a translation of a lecture series by Martin Heidegger, first published as *Grundbegriffe* by Vittorio Klostermann in 1981 (*Gesamtausgabe*, vol. 51). Heidegger conducted these lectures during the winter semester of 1941. This places them within the phase of his thinking that has become known as the "turning" (*Kehre*), a phase generally recognized to begin with the essay "On the Essence of Truth" (1930) and to culminate in the "Letter on Humanism" (1946). The "turning" is a transition beyond the fundamental ontology of *Being and Time,* where the temporality of Dasein is to provide a hermeneutical basis for interpreting the meaning of being. In the transition, Heidegger shifts from the problematic of the meaning of being to the question of the truth of being, a truth whose disclosure is to be won through a confrontation with the history of being itself, instead of the existential analyses of Dasein that constitute his earlier work.

This confrontation is an attempt to recover something of the original experience of being in the "first inception" of Western thought, i.e., in the texts of the pre-Socratic philosophers. However, since an inception is by its very nature unique and beyond duplication, any recovery of the "first inception" must be an "other inception."[1] It also must be original and unique, and so cannot be a mere reiteration of ancient Greek thinking. Thus Heidegger seeks to confront these Greek texts, e.g., the fragment of Anaximander, in a way that is also "new." This is the ultimate design of the lectures.

Before carrying out the attempt at an "other inception" of the history of being, Heidegger sets up the problematic in a series of preceding moments. (They are indicated by the division headings inserted into the text by the editor of *Grundbegriffe,* Petra Jaeger.) These moments are united as an attempt to follow an ancient saying, "μελέτα τὸ πᾶν," which Heidegger translates as "take into care beings as a whole." Although Heidegger himself does not name the source of this saying, it is historically attributed to Periander, one of the "seven wise men" of ancient Greece.[2] It has traditionally been understood to mean that the wise concern themselves with the whole, while the unwise concern themselves with only a part of the whole. In other words, the wise consider everything in its totality, but the unwise pursue only their own partial interests. Furthermore, *Melete* (Care or Practice) is one of the original muses, along with *Mneme* (Memory) and *Aoide* (Song).[3] These original muses are essential aspects of poetry. *Melete* has been interpreted as the discipline and practice necessary to learn the art, *Mneme* as the retention required for recitation and improvisation, and *Aoide* as the poetic song itself, the culmination of the other two aspects.[4] In the earliest tradition of Greek thinking, care, remembrance, and song were understood as religious powers. For Heidegger, their significance is ontological—they are aspects of the "saying" of being (assuming we interpret "song" to mean "saying" in its poetic, revelatory mode). These connections are apparent in Heidegger's interpretation of the saying of Periander.

The first moment is an attempt to follow this saying by considering the whole of beings in light of the difference between beings and being. It raises the issue of this difference in terms of its unsatisfactory treatment in traditional logic and metaphysics, as well as its apparent meaninglessness for ordinary common sense. Heidegger suggests that there is a more fundamental experience of being than the metaphysical tradition or common sense would acknowledge, and that this experience is hinted at in a series of "guidewords." These guidewords emerge from the paradoxical conclusions about being that result from traditional and commonsensical modes of reasoning: e.g., "Being is the emptiest and at the same time a surplus; Being is the most common and at the same time unique," etc. These are not to be taken as "propositions" about being, but as indications that point beyond propositional thought altogether.

The guidewords show that we are privy to a fundamental experience of being that escapes our formal and everyday habits of thinking, for these are oriented upon beings alone, while being, and the difference between being and beings, remain forgotten. The paradoxical nature of the guidewords is not to discourage further thought, as if labeling them is already a sufficient indication of the underlying experience they signify. Nor are their oppositions to be resolved dialectically, such that their tension is overcome at a higher level of synthesis. Rather, Heidegger sees in these oppositions an opening into the fundamental experience of being itself. This discussion constitutes the second moment of the lectures.

The third moment is a reflection upon the relationship between man and being, a relationship implied and rendered problematical by the inadequacies of traditional reasoning vis-à-vis the experience of being these inadequacies already hint at. To recover an original experience of being we must attain a more original experience of ourselves. That means we must overcome our tendency to see ourselves as just another being in the totality of beings. We must instead remember that being addresses us and no other being, and that this address is a unique occurrence that distinguishes us among beings.

Being's address to us, and our responses, are the history of being itself. Even our turning away from being toward beings is a response to being. Indeed, this is the history of the "first inception," whose legacy is metaphysics—the conception of being *only* as the being of beings, and the conception of humanity as just another being (the rational animal) among others. But the fact that our response *can be* such a turning away from being, or a casting away of being, shows that our relationship to being is more intimate and more immediate than any relationship to ourselves or to other beings. For only in turning away from being are we confronted with beings, including ourselves, in the first place. Heidegger characterizes this relationship to being as the difference between being and beings, and he tries to disclose it as our original abode or place of residence.

We reside in the place where we bring the temporal coming and going of beings to a stand, where a world (the totality of beings) takes shape and things become understood and familiar. However, our original relationship to being, to what we turn away from for the sake of the familiar, remains strange and unfamiliar. Nevertheless, it is the "ground" of our historical interpretation of beings, including ourselves, and is therefore the "origin" of history; it is "historicality" *per se*. As such an origin it is an inception—

what is prior to any merely historical "beginning." Heidegger attempts to recover (remember) the experience of this inception through an interpretation of the Anaximander fragment. This interpretation, which is also a translation, is the fourth and final moment of the lectures.

The traditional source for this fragment (B1 in Diels/Kranz) is a fragment from a work by Theophrastus entitled *Opinions of the Physicists* (Φυσικῶν δόχαι), as cited by Simplicius's commentary on Aristotle's *Physics* (*Physics* 24, 13).[5] In Diels/Kranz, part A, the fragment begins with line 13 of Simplicius: "Anaximander . . . says . . . that the ἄπειρον is the principle of existing things . . . and that from which existing things come into being is that into which destruction too happens," etc. Other versions, such as the one given in Kirk and Raven, are also taken from Simplicius but begin at line 17: " . . . according to necessity. For they pay penalty and retribution to each other for their injustice according to the assessment of Time."[6] They assume that only the latter passage belongs to Anaximander, while the preceding lines about γένεσίς and φϑορά (coming to be and passing away) are an interpretative gloss by Theophrastus, a peripatetic philosopher.

In the present lectures, Heidegger not only accepts the citation in Diels/Kranz part A, where the entire passage from Simplicius is given, but also divides it into two "sayings." The main fragment is indeed the one given in Diels/Kranz B1, beginning with "that from which existing things come into being," etc. But Heidegger also extracts the first passage in Simplicius (line 13) and rephrases it as a second saying of Anaximander: "the ἄπειρον is the principle of all existing things." Thus he attributes to Anaximander a passage that Diels and Kranz attribute to Simplicius and excise from the fragment in B1. Moreover, he brings in this "second" saying of Anaximander to guide his interpretation of the main fragment, and he reads the first passage of the main fragment (arguably from Theophrastus) as the basis for interpreting the remainder. Just what is at stake for Heidegger in taking these philological risks is a matter that cannot be addressed here. It is interesting to note, however, that when he deals with the Anaximander fragment again in 1946 he accepts only the minimal version (as found, e.g., in Kirk and Raven) as authentic.[7]

As Heidegger reminds us, every translation is already an interpretation. In what follows I have attempted to translate and interpret Heidegger's text in terms of both its merely historical circumstances and its truly historical subject matter. Excluding the treatment of the Anaximander fragment, Heidegger's German is informal and colloquial. I have attempted to allow its conversational tone to emerge as much as possible, fully aware that colloquialisms are notoriously difficult and dangerous for any translator. The discussion of the Anaximander fragment presents its own dangers, especially since Heidegger exploits certain root-connections among words, connections that do not duplicate in English. In some cases I have indicated these by including the original German in brackets, but I have kept such cases to a minimum in order to preserve a sense of natural English throughout the whole. Nevertheless, there are certain terms that presented special obstacles for translation and I will note them here.

Heidegger's translation of the Anaximander fragment is difficult, not only because of its duplication of Greek syntax but also because of Heidegger's original interpretation of key terms. For example, he translates ἀρχή as *Verfügung,* δίκη as *Fug,* and ἀδικία as *Unfug*—which I have rendered as "enjoinment," "the fit," and "the unfit." I have chosen these terms to emphasize the sense of jointure that links these words in Heidegger's German. Furthermore, where the text speaks of "overcoming the unfit," it should be noted that the word Heidegger uses for "overcoming" is *verwinden,* a term that is also used for "getting over" something—e.g., an illness or a tragic experience. Thus it does not mean to overcome in the sense of conquest or annihilation, but in the sense of passing through and beyond. This is also consonant with Heidegger's sense of being as "transition" (*Übergang*), which is the culminating moment in his interpretation of Anaximander. A more complete list of key German terms and their English translations is provided in the Glossary.

Where possible, I have provided the standard English translations for passages from other authors quoted by Heidegger, Nietzsche being the most frequent example. I have not, however, updated Heidegger's German references. Aside from the question as to whether such updating is warranted under the specific provisions of the *Gesamtausgabe,* there is a special problem with Heidegger's citations from Nietzsche's *Will to Power*. While the Colli and Montinari editions of Nietzsche's works are now standard German references, these editors do not recognize *Der Wille zur Macht* as an authentic text, and have dispersed the aphorisms once collected under that heading back into the *Nachlass*. This makes reference to Colli and Montinari impractical for dealing with those passages from the *Will to Power* cited by Heidegger. Thus I have retained all of the references as they appear in the *Gesamtausgabe*. Additional remarks by the translator are appended in square brackets, which also set off translator's insertions—most often of German words—in the body of the text. The numbers in the running heads refer to the pagination of the German edition. The articulation of the text into parts, divisions, and numbered sections and the formulation of titles for them were contributed by Petra Jaeger.

I would like to thank John Sallis of Vanderbilt University and Janet Rabinowitch of Indiana University Press for their support during all phases of this project, and Hugh J. Silverman of the State University of New York at Stony Brook for encouraging me to undertake it in the first place. I would also like to thank Ursula Bernis for her helpful suggestions during the initial stages of the translation, and Robert Barford of Eastern Illinois University for his help in identifying the saying of Periander as well as the sources for the Anaximander fragment. Finally, I am greatly indebted to Thomas Nenon of the University of Memphis, who thoroughly reviewed the manuscript and made innumerable corrections and suggestions for improvement. I have incorporated all of the former and the vast majority of the latter into the text. Needless to say, I alone am responsible for any deficiencies that remain.

GARY E. AYLESWORTH

NOTES

1. For an extended treatment of the relation between the "first inception" and the "other inception" see Martin Heidegger, *Beiträge zur Philosophie (Vom Er-*

eignis), Gesamtausgabe 65 (Frankfurt am Main: Klostermann, 1989), especially sections 89–100.

2. See Diels/Kranz, *Die Fragmente der Vorsokratiker,* vol. 1, 12th ed. (Dublin/ Zurich: Weidmann, 1966), p. 65.

3. As recounted in Pausanias, *Description of Greece,* IX 29, 2–3. Loeb Classical Library Edition, vol. IV, pp. 294/295.

4. See Marcel Detienne, *Les maîtres de vérité dans la grèce archaïque* (Paris: F. Maspero, 1967), pp. 11–12.

5. See Simplicii, *In Aristotelis Physicorum Libros Quattor Priores Commentaria,* ed. H. Diels (Berlin: G. Reimer), 1882, vol. IX, in *Commentaria in Aristoteliem Graeca,* ed. Academiae Litterarum Reggiae Borrusicae (Berlin: G. Reimer), 1882–1909, pp. 24, 17ff.

6. See G. S. Kirk and J. E. Raven, *The Presocratic Philosophers* (Cambridge: Cambridge University Press, 1962), p. 117.

7. See Martin Heidegger, "The Anaximander Fragment" in *Early Greek Thinking: The Dawn of Western Philosophy,* trans. David Farrell Krell and Frank A. Capuzzi (New York: Harper & Row, 1975), pp. 13–58.

INTRODUCTION

The Internal Connection between Ground–Being–Inception

§1. Elucidation of the title of the lecture "Basic Concepts"

a) Basic concepts are *ground*-concepts

"Basic Concepts" [*Grundbegriffe*]—of what? The title of this lecture does not say. Hence what is supposed to be grasped by these concepts remains unclear. "Concepts" are said to be representations [*Vorstellungen*] in which we bring before ourselves an object or entire regions of objects in general. "*Basic* Concepts" [*Grund*begriffe], then, are more general representations of the most possibly encompassing regions. Such regions are nature, history, "the" state, "the" law, humanity, animal, or whatever else. However, in the lecture's title there is no talk of the basic concepts of nature, of art, and other regions. The title does not specify anything of the kind for which the "Basic Concepts" are supposed to be such basic concepts, whether for the investigation of art history or jurisprudence, for chemistry or mechanical engineering, or for any other "subject area" or field of human practice. Perhaps the unsupplemented title "Basic Concepts" means this: that it does not treat of particular regions of beings, nor of the corresponding sciences that investigate them individually.

Since, however, the lecture is listed under the "rubric" "philosophy," 'naturally' the basic concepts "of philosophy" are meant. But if these were meant it would have been stated. Instead, the title only says "Basic Concepts," not "*The* Basic Concepts" nor "the" basic concepts of philosophy.

According to the traditional and also correct view, philosophy indeed thinks something more general than the particular regions of nature, history, state, art, nation, living thing. If we do not intend to mean the basic concepts of philosophy, then the unsupplemented title must have something even more general in mind than what is thought in "philosophy." This most-general-of-all supposedly does not allow itself to be said directly. Perhaps there are no words with sufficient naming power to do so; perhaps the "appropriate" words are so used up they do not say anything anymore. Hence such an indefinite title is perhaps well suited, for thus we do not commit ourselves to anything in advance.

On the other hand, this nondescript title has a peculiar decisiveness about it. Evidently nothing arbitrary or peripheral is spoken of here, but only what is necessary and pertains to the main issue. But why isn't this said directly? Well, it is. We only have to listen in the right way. With the first apprehension of the title, we must immediately begin to practice what will be demanded of us from now on: relinquishing the customary, which is at the same time the comfortable. We have to assume an attitude whose achievement requires no special knowledge in advance, neither scientific nor philosophical. The latter may be useful for other purposes, but here such knowledge would only be a hindrance. For here only one thing is required: readiness to put the essence of man at risk in thinking that which grounds this essence, and, foremost, that which grounds everything that man takes for being. Whatever grounds everything and gives ground to everything is itself the ground.

Thus the title tells us something about what is to be comprehended there after all. We only have to write the word differently: *Ground-Concepts* [*Grund-Begriffe*]. Now the title says "the ground" is to be conceived, grasped, seized, indeed first reached, indeed first only anticipated. We think toward the ground of everything.

We are not, as it might appear, dealing with "concepts" as such—with much-maligned "mere concepts," from which we easily recoil, though we assure ourselves at the same time that they are nothing concrete and lead nowhere.

b) The claim of the ground-concepts

"*Ground-Concepts*" calls for us to grasp the ground, reach the foundation. This title calls us to come to stand where a footing and a permanence are granted, where all decisions are made, but also from where all indecisiveness borrows its hiding places. Grasping the ground means reaching the ground of everything in an understanding that not only takes notice of something but is, as a knowing, a standing and a stance. Knowing the ground is more originary, that is, more far-reaching than common understanding. But more originary also means more decisive than every usual "willing," and more intimate than every familiar "feeling." Therefore knowing the ground does not first need a "character" in order to have stability. This knowing *is* character itself. It is that stamp of man without which all firmness of will remains blind stubbornness, all deeds mere fleeting successes, all action a self-consuming busyness, and all "experiences" self-delusions.

"*Ground-Concepts*," that sounds more like a claim [*Anspruch*] upon us. We are exhorted [*angesprochen*] to set our thinking upon the path of reflection. From the time when the essential configuration of Western history (and not the mere succession of events) begins to unfold, a saying is handed down to us that goes μελέτα τὸ πᾶν, "Take into care beings as a whole" [*das Seiende im Ganzen*]—that means, consider that everything depends upon the whole of beings, upon what addresses [*anspricht*] humanity from there. Always consider the essential, first and last, and assume the attitude that matures us for such reflection. Like everything essential, this attitude must be simple, and the suggestion that intimates this attitude (which is a knowing) to us must be simple as well. It suffices for this suggestion to distinguish what humanity, having come to itself, must attend to.

c) The difference of claims upon man

α) The claim of requirements: Needing

We attend either to what we need or to what we can do without.

We measure what we need according to our requirements, according to desires left to themselves and their cravings, according to what we count with and count upon. Behind these desires and cravings stands the press of that unrest for which every "enough" is just as soon a "never enough." This unrest of continuously new needing, of self-increasing and expanding "interests," does not originate from anything like an artificially cultivated avarice. Rather, this avidity is already the result of that unrest within which the surge of mere life, of the merely living, reveals itself. To remain thrust and forced into its own craving belongs to the essence of the living. Indeed, "the living," which we know as plants and animals, always seems to find and maintain its fixed shape precisely in this craving, whereas man can expressly elevate the living and its cravings into a guiding measure and make of it the "principle" of "progress." If we attend only to what we need, we are yoked into the compulsive unrest of mere life. This form of life arouses the appearance of the moved and the self-moving, and therefore of the free. Thus the appearance of freedom exists precisely where man attends only to what he needs. For man's calculating and planning move within a field of play whose limits he himself can adjust to his particular wants.

However, this way man is only "free," i.e., mobile, within the compulsion of his "life-interests." He is, in certain respects, unfettered within the circuit of compulsion, which determines itself from the premise that everything is a matter of utility. Servitude under the dominion of the constantly "needed," i.e., of utility, looks like the freedom and magnificence of consumption [Nutzniessung] and its increase.

β) The claim upon the essence of historical man

Man attends either to what he needs or to what he can do without.

In this other attitude, he does not calculate under the compulsion of utility and from the unrest of consumption. He does not calculate at all, but considers everything from a standpoint that is limited to the essential. This limitation is only an apparent restriction, in truth it is a release into the expanse of those demands that befit man's essence. Attending to the dispensable brings man into the simplicity and unequivocalness of an entirely different domain. Here speak claims that do not derive from his needs and do not pertain to the prospect of the well-being of the individual and the many. This domain alone is the site in which a "realm"

[*Reich*] can be founded. For here alone historical man can stand out into an openness while subordinating everything needful and useful to himself, thereby first becoming capable of ruling in an essential sense.

Man, in his essence, is addressed by claims that demand an answer. But these claims, which we better name exhortations [*An-sprechungen*], cannot be displayed like matters of fact, nor enumerated like priorities. Historical man must be struck by them, and for that he must allow himself to be struck in the first place. Perhaps the old saying μελέτα τὸ πᾶν puts something into words that strikes historical man in his essence, such that all that is merely human is not sufficient to satisfy the claim.

Perhaps the attempt to think "*Ground-Concepts*," to reach the ground of everything, comes to a knowing that cannot be added up from knowledge about "life," nor from the results of science, nor from the doctrines of a "faith." Presumably, also, an individual can never invent such a knowing from the fortuitousness of his abilities and endowments. He can foist such knowledge neither upon himself nor upon others by decree. The relation to the essential, wherein historical man becomes free, can have its origin only within the essential itself.

d) Readiness for the originary, the incipient, and the "knowing better" of historiological consciousness

Man is either ready for what is always original, or he knows better.

Knowing better also reigns where man seems to subjugate himself to a divine world-plan. This knowing better begins in Western history with the advent of the age of historiological [*historischen*] consciousness. The rise and universal currency of historiological science and its varied utilization and exploitation, however, are already the late development of man's calculating "attitude" toward history. This attitude begins with the ascendancy of Christianity as a principle for shaping the "world." Since man has become ever more ingenious and clever in the last centuries so that nothing escapes him, the relation to the essential is more and more covered over, or, what is even more portentous, is reckoned into the otherwise calculable. There arises a condition in which everything is gauged according to whether it is new or old. In general, what counts for unlimited historiological calculation as "new" is not only the hitherto unfamiliar and unprecedented, but also everything that continues and promotes whatever progression happens to be under way. What is useless in relation to the promotion of progress counts as "old." The old is then the antiquated. Thus in each epoch historiology and historiological research endeavor, always under different catchwords, to "paint" over the old and the bygone with the gloss of the respective present, and so to justify historiological activity itself as indispensable.

However, the essential has its own history [*Geschichte*] and is not calculable according to the ciphers "new" and "old." Where such calculation nevertheless occurs, relations to the essential are most covered over. There man stubbornly sets himself against the demand that he reach the essential upon the path of remembrance [*Erinnerung*] and that he grasp the ground. According to the view of the merely calculating man, remembrance fixes itself to something earlier, hence older, hence old, hence antiquated, and therefore at best attainable through extant historiological research. Yet the earlier, assuming it is essential, remains outside that utility to which everything "new" and "old" in the conventional sense must subject itself.

e) The meaning of reflection upon the inception of history

According to the historiological reckoning of time the earliest is indeed the oldest, and, in the estimation of ordinary understanding, also the most antiquated. The earliest, however, can also be the first according to rank and wealth, according to originality and bindingness for our history [*Geschichte*] and impending historical [*geschichtliche*] decisions. The first in this essential sense *for us* is *the Greeks*. We name this "earliest" *the incipient* [*das Anfängliche*]. From it comes an exhortation, in relation to which the opining of the individual and the many fails to hear, and misconstrues its essential power, unaware of the unique opportunity: that remembrance of the inception can transport us into the essential.

We can fail to hear the claim of the incipient. That it comes to this seems to alter nothing in the course of our history. Thus the dispensability of remembering the inception is "practically" demonstrated. Indeed, we can not only fail to hear the claim of the incipient, but even drive ourselves to the self-delusion that we do not have to listen to it in the first place, since we already "know" about it. The whole world talks about the extraordinary "cultural" significance of the ancient Greeks. But no one who speaks like this has the slightest knowledge that, and how, an inception occurs there.

Those who evince a somewhat belated enthusiasm for "classical antiquity," and likewise those who encourage and promote the "humanistic *gymnasium*," demonstrate a no more essential stance toward the incipient, so long as their efforts are devoted only to salvaging what has been hitherto; so long as they fall back upon an inherited and very questionably arranged cultural treasure, and in so doing consider themselves superior to the enthusiasts of the technological age. Familiarity with the ancient Greek language is certainly indispensable for the endeavor, expressly understood as a task, to awaken, develop, and secure remembrance of the incipient. The education of those who must bring about remembrance of the incipient cannot forgo instruction in the language of the ancient Greeks. But one should not infer from this the erroneous opinion that those who, for whatever reasons and intentions, possess knowledge of the Greek language and pursue a "humanistic schooling" would also be in possession of the ancient Greek world. Not all of those who study at a humanistic *gymnasium*, nor all of those who teach there, nor all who train these teachers at the university, have already, by reason of that fact, a knowledge of the inception of the essential in Western history, and that means of its future.

How many Germans "live" who speak their mother tongue effortlessly and yet are unable to understand Kant's *Critique of Pure Reason* or one of Hölderlin's hymns! Hence whoever has mastered the Greek language, or has some acquaintance with it by accident or choice, possesses not the least proof thereby that he is able to think *according to* the thought of a Greek thinker. For it could be that he does not let himself get involved with questions in the first place, since he imagines himself, perhaps as an adherent of a religious faith, to be in possession of the truth. In such cases, which are not at all rare, passion for the "classical" and for "humanism" is even more fateful than naked ignorance of this "cultural treasure." Love of antiquity is then a pretext for striving to evade every decisive reflection.

Readiness to confront the inception of our history thus remains more vital than any knowledge of languages. This means readiness to confront the essential, which, as a decision, is projected ahead of this history at its inception, and is its ground.

Readiness to confront the inception can originate as genuine only from the necessities of the history into which we ourselves are placed. When we cast aside reflection upon the necessary and insist we are in possession of the truth, all remembrance of the inception is impossible. And where such remembrance does seem to be fostered, it is only an evasion of what is worthy of question and a flight into the past.

The measure of whether remembrance of the inception is genuine can never be determined from an interest in reviving classical antiquity, but only from a resolve to attain an essential knowing that holds for what is to come. This knowing need not even concern the inception of our history at first.

The test, however, of whether we are merely collecting information, whether we are merely taking bygone cultural aims as a pretext for thoughtlessness, or whether we are willing to set out upon the path to reflection, this test we must put to ourselves. To this belongs inner freedom, but also the opportunity to experience first of all how such reflection proceeds and what it entails.

f) The goal of the lecture: Reflection as preparation for confronting the inception of our history

This lecture aims to provide the opportunity for such reflection or experience. You should think according to and along with what is here thought forth. This thinking is not prescribed in any examination protocol, and fortunately cannot be so prescribed. Such thinking does not belong to any "required course of study." Indeed, it does not belong to any "course of study" at all. It also does not serve to further "general education." It cannot provide entertainment for students of all departments. The thinking in which we reflect and do nothing but reflect does not yield any utility whatsoever, for it allows us to recognize that there *is* something that does not have to be "effective" or useful in order to *be*. Therefore in this thinking we are left to our own freedom.

The possibilities for professional training, the appropriation of the skills necessary for this, instruction in areas of knowledge not directly relevant to professional training, these can always be subsequently obtained and improved upon where needed. By contrast, the moments for essential reflection are rare and unrepeatable. That holds above all for those moments that occur once in a lifetime that either awaken, bury, or waste one's fundamental abilities for the entire future.

"*Ground-Concepts*"—this title involves the readiness to reach the ground and not to let it go again. If this readiness is not to remain an empty curiosity, it must immediately begin practicing what it is ready for. It must begin with reflection.

It is now time to actually carry out a simple reflection, in which we shall prepare to confront the inception of our history. From such remembrance of this inception we can come to anticipate that history is moving toward decisions that will surpass everything otherwise familiar to modern man in his objectives. If this is the case, then it is necessary at this moment of the world for the Germans to know what could be demanded of them in the future, when the "spirit of their fatherland" must be a "holy heart of nations" [*Völker*].

Recapitulation

1. Our understanding of "basic concepts" and our relation to them as an anticipatory knowing

By "basic concepts" one usually understands those notions that delimit a region of objects as a whole, or according to single, leading aspects. Thus the concept of "force" is a basic concept of natural science, the concept of "culture" is a basic concept of historiology, the concept "law" is a basic concept of jurisprudence—in another way also a basic concept of natural science—, the concept of "style" is a basic concept of research in art history, but also in "philology." Indeed, it originates from here, as it first means the mode of writing and then of saying and speaking, and finally pertains to the "formal language" of each "work," which concerns the historians of plastic art and painting, indeed all "aesthetics."

So understood, basic concepts assist the particular sciences with the investigation of their regions as guidelines for questioning, answering, and presenting.

We now take more literally the title of this lecture, according to which the first elucidation was given. We write it correspondingly: *Ground-Concepts*. The title expresses the demand to reach the ground of all that is, of what can therefore be called beings, or to anticipate it and not to let what is anticipated go again.

We are thus concerned solely with attaining the ground and the relation to the ground, not with becoming acquainted with "concepts" as mere casings of representations. The relation to the ground is also already a knowing, even where it is a matter of essential anticipation [*Ahnen*]. And anticipation of the essential [*Wesenhaft*] always remains more vital [*wesentlich*] than any certainty in calculating what is without essence [*Wesenlos*].

If we are talking here about anticipation, we should not substitute a rambling feeling of incidental states of mind for the concept and its rigor. The word anticipation should show us the way to consider that what should be brought to knowing here cannot be produced from man by his own choice. Anticipation means grasping something that comes upon us, whose coming has long held sway, except that we overlook it. And indeed we overlook it simply because our knowing attitude as a whole remains confused and does not recognize the simplest differences, or mistakes or ignores the import of differences that are known. Thinking in anticipation and for anticipation is essentially more rigorous and exacting than any formal-conceptual cleverness in whatever sector of the calculable.

To attain anticipatory knowing we must practice such knowing. The fundamental condition for such practice is not a prior familiarity, for example, in the form of philosophical opinions acquired through reading. The fundamental condition is readiness to make ourselves free for the essential. Mere familiarity, whether narrow or wide, is capable of nothing by itself. However, that does not mean we can do without familiarity everywhere and completely, especially mature and carefully cultivated familiarity. Nor that its possession belongs to the long elapsed ideals of an "intellectualistic" era. Thinking that merely looks to the useful first notices gaps and mistakes only when it comes to harm, when lack of those who are capable and knowledgeable endangers the mastery of present and future tasks.

2. The decay of knowing in the present age: The decision in favor of the useful over what we can do without

The store of knowledge that today's youth bring with them corresponds neither to the greatness nor to the seriousness of the task. Knowing is equal to the task of the "age" in only one respect: its decay and its task are equally enormous.

But these deficiencies will not be eliminated by suddenly beginning to learn more and faster. We must first begin again to learn "learning" and to know standards of measure. Cultural dissolution will not be abated by the mere introduction of newer and more convenient "textbooks." The youth must not wait until more fundamental acquaintance and actual contemplation are demanded of them from above, for it is precisely the other way around. It is the prerogative of a true and wakeful youth to develop exhortations to knowledge from out of itself, and to cling to these exhortations for itself, in order to construct the future. Whether one occasionally "reads a book" is a measure for the petite bourgeoisie. It does not ask whether today's man, who gets his "education" from "charts" and "magazines," from radio reports and movie theaters, whether such a confused, dizzy, and purely American man still knows, or can know, what "reading" means.

Nor will the degeneration of knowing be overcome when one merely declares how much better it was in the old days. For even the former school and educational system of the last decades was already no longer able to awaken and keep awake the binding power of spirit and the bindingness of the essential, and thus no longer able to force us into reflection. In times of essential decisions a comfortable retreat to what has been up to now helps as little as the hurried restriction to daily needs. Here only reflection saves us, and the inner choice as to whether we want to be exposed to the claim the essential makes upon us or not. The decision as to whether we are capable of making decisions about ourselves comes before everything. If we are, then the decision is whether we adhere to what we need or attend to what we can do without.

If we adhere to what we need, that means, in your present case, chasing after what is necessary for the most convenient possible arrangement of professional training.

By comparison, if we attend at the same time to what we can do without, when, as for many of our young friends at the front, it comes to the most extreme, then what alone remains essential comes into view almost of itself.

The mark of what we decide here does not consist in the fact that some enroll in a philosophy course and others do not. How the aforementioned decision is made, and if it is made, no one can establish immediately from any kind of mark or certificate. Here each person is responsible for himself, for his own delusions, and that for which he holds himself ready.

Thus one can note this reference to the crisis of knowing, grounded actually in the essence of modern history and not produced by the present emergency, with a certain satisfaction that such a thing is said. Such a one takes his misplaced smirk over this criticism already for an accomplishment. However, one then leaves everything the way it was, not wishing to know that what is at risk here is not the organization of the teaching system, but the most proper concern of youth: that it must take things into its own hands, that the best organization and the best curricula do not help here, because behind all of these stand decisions about what is essential. Whoever thinks he can find confirmations of his own decisionless discontent here is living in an illusion.

3. The inception as a decision about what is essential in Western history (in modern times: unconditional will and technology)

Of course it is especially difficult for modern man to find his way into the essential, because in another respect he is familiar with too much and indeed believes he is familiar with everything. For him everything earlier is something past, by means of which he can illuminate what comes later and what pertains to him according to his needs. Here the earlier has no power of decision because it is no longer experienced as the incipient in history. The inception, however, can only be experienced as an inception when we ourselves think inceptively and essentially. This inception is not the past, but rather, because it has decided in advance everything to come, it is constantly of the future. We must think about the inception this way.

By inception we understand the originary decisions that sustain in advance what is essential in Western history. To the essential first belongs the determination of the essence of truth, in whose light Western man seeks, finds, secures, and transforms what is true.

The inception as the inception of history is only where there is freedom, that means where a humanity decisively comports itself toward beings and their truth. Nations and races can perhaps live without history if it is a matter of mere "life." The mere passage of "life" is not yet history, not even when much "happens," i.e., transpires, in it.

The inception of our history is the Greeks. We see here something essential that harbors still uncompleted decisions within itself. For us this inception is not "antiquity," and reflection upon it is not an activity aimed merely at salvaging a handed-down cultural treasure. The thinker of history Jakob Burckhardt (who, happily, was never a "historian") said decades ago: Occupation with antiquity "is treated here and there like a poor old relative, who, for decency's sake, one may not allow to go under."[1]

The equipment needed for reflection upon the inception is, for the purpose of this lecture, directly necessary only for the person who is attempting to provide an opportunity for reflection for the first time here. Where it is necessary for us to hear the Greek word of ancient sayings, translation can be sufficient—to be sure, under the condition that the elucidation of what the word says to us is not lacking, that it is thought

---

1. J. Burckhardt, *Weltgeschichtliche Betrachtungen*, Ges. Ausg. vol. VII: *Historische Fragmente aus dem Nachlaß*, ed. A. Oeri and E. Durr (Berlin and Leipzig, 1929), p. 229.

through within the horizon of our own experiencing and knowing. Besides, the German language is suited like no other for translating the ancient Greek word, especially when the Greek word is not merely translated into a current German usage, but when this too is renewed at the same time and becomes incipient itself.

But what actually distances modern man from the inception of his history is not only and not primarily the other "language," but the changed mode of world-interpretation and the basic position in the midst of beings. The modern position is the "technological." It is not technological because there are steam engines and then the combustion motor, but there are these things because the epoch is technological. What we call modern technology is not only a tool and a means, over and against which today's man can be a master or servant. Before and beyond these possible attitudes, technology is an already decided mode of world-interpretation, which determines not only the means of transportation, subsistence, and recreation but also the possibilities for any human attitude whatsoever. It preforms them according to their capacity for implementation. That is why technology is mastered only where it is affirmed from the outset and without reservation. That means the practical mastery of technology in its unconditional development already presupposes a metaphysical subjugation to technology. Accompanying this subjugation within us is an attitude that grasps everything according to plan and calculation, and does so with a view to vast time-spans in order willfully and knowingly to secure what can last for the longest possible duration.

It is one thing when empires endure for millennia because of their continuing stability. It is something else when world dominions are knowingly planned to last millennia and the assurance of their existence is undertaken by *that* will whose essential goal is the greatest possible duration of the greatest possible order of the largest possible masses. This will has been the concealed metaphysical essence of modernity for the last three centuries. It appears in various predecessors and guises that are not sure of themselves and their essence. That in the twentieth century this will would attain the shape of the unconditional, Nietzsche had clearly thought through in advance. Participation in this will to man's unconditional mastery over the earth, and the execution of this will, harbor within themselves that subjugation to technology that does not appear as resistance and resentment. That subjection appears as will, and that means it is also effective here.

However, where one interprets the execution of this metaphysical will as a "product" of selfishness and the caprice of "dictators" and "authoritarian states," there speak only political calculation and propaganda, or the metaphysical naivete of a thinking that ran aground centuries ago, or both. Political circumstances, economic situations, population growth, and the like, can be the proximate causes and horizons for carrying out this metaphysical will of modern world-history. But they are never the ground of this history and therefore never its "end." The will to preservation, and that always means the will to enhance life and its lastingness, works essentially against decline and sees deficiency and powerlessness in what lasts only a short while.

On the contrary, for the inception of our history, for the Greeks, decline was unique, momentary, laudable, and great. Clearly, we have to distinguish here between decline while entering into something unique, and perishing while clinging fast to the ordinary. What is imperishable in the inception does not consist in the longest possible duration of its consequences nor in the furthest possible extension and breadth of its effects, but in the rarity and singularity of each varied return of what is originary within it. Hence we cannot experience the inception through mere historiological familiarity with what was before, but only in realizing what essentially came to be known at the inception itself.

4. Practicing the relation to what is "thought-worthy" by considering the ground

If now and then we hear a brief saying of the incipient Greek thinkers of the West, the important thing at first is that *we* hear, and we think about the fact that everything has to do with *us*. But in order to consider this, we must actually become practiced in thinking. The worst way to practice thinking, however, would be an academic course in "logic." The usual, orthodox logic thinks, at best (if it thinks at all), "about" thinking. But we do not learn to think originarily when someone shows us how to think, in an inferior and long-since impossible manner, "about" thinking. Rather, we learn to think only when we try to attain an essential and genuine relation to what above all else is thought-*worthy*. And what is thoughtworthy is certainly not "thinking" but what challenges thinking, what places thinking in its service and thus bestows rank and value upon it. We do not learn this essential thinking by means of any "logic."

"Ground-Concepts" means to say: grasping the ground of everything, and that means to attain a relation to the "ground" of everything. What "ground" means here must be clarified step by step, along with what the relation to the ground consists in, to what extent a knowing belongs to this relation, and to what extent this relation is even itself a knowing. Thus it would be premature if we wanted to equate "ground" with "cause" of everything, and wanted furthermore to interpret this cause as a first cause in the sense of a creator according to the Bible and Christian dogma. It would also be premature to believe that with these "concepts" it is solely a matter of representing the ground. It is rather a question of extending our thinking toward the manner in which the ground includes us in its essence, not the manner in which we take the ground to be merely an "object" and use it for an "explanation of the world."

However the essence of the ground, but also "the concepts," i.e., the relation to the ground, might explain and confirm themselves to us, one thing remains clear in advance: no individual with a worked-out doctrine and viewpoint can arbitrarily, at any particular time, expound something and decide it by decree. It is also easy to see that an examination of previous viewpoints and doctrines concerning the "ground" and the "relation" to the "ground" at best provides a "historiological" familiarity and avoids precisely what is all-important: the relation through which we ourselves come into proximity with what strikes us essentially and makes a claim upon us. We do not wish to discuss doctrines. Rather, we want to become aware of the essential, in which we stand, or within which we are perhaps still driven to and fro without a footing and without understanding.

5. The essential admittance of historical man into the inception, into the "essence" of ground

We must listen our way into that place where we ourselves belong. With this, reflection leads us through the question as to whether we still belong anywhere at all. Even to merely anticipate where we could belong it is necessary to experience ourselves. This means "ourselves" not according to an historiologically given condition, "ourselves" not according to a currently existing situation, "ourselves" not according to the individually occurring specimens of humanity, but "ourselves" in respect to what determines us and is other than us, which nevertheless governs our essence. We call this, arbitrarily at first, the inception of our history. By this we do not mean history as a series of events in terms of a "causal nexus," of which what occurs later and today is an effect. History means, again at first appearance arbitrarily, *the happening [Ereignis] of a decision about the essence of truth.* The manner in which the whole of beings is revealed, in which man is allowed to stand in the midst of this revelation, is grounded and transformed in such a decision. Such a happening is exceptional, and this exceptional history is so simple when it happens and prepares itself that man at first and for a long time thereafter fails to see it and fails to recognize it. This is because his vision is confused by habituation to the multiplicity of the ordinary.

The simple is the most difficult, and can only be experienced after long endeavor. Remembrance of the inception of our history is the awakening of knowing about the decision that, even now, and in the future, determines Western humanity. Remembrance of the inception is therefore not a flight into the past but readiness for what is to come.

In such remembrance we ourselves stand everywhere at risk, for in remembrance we always remain unimportant as extant human specimens and currently existing human groups. Historical man matters only when and insofar as he stands in relation to the essence of history and hears a claim from this essence according to which what matters is distinguished from what doesn't matter, i.e., the groundless. Above all we ourselves stand at risk, and that means the truth that determines us and has perhaps long since become unrecognizable. But we do not find ourselves by becoming selfish and following the impulse of those interests that merely drive us along. We are most likely to find ourselves when we succeed in looking away from what is self-seeking and peculiar to ourselves and bring into relief something long overlooked. Let us allow ourselves, then, to be struck by the incipient, and come to hear an ancient saying.

Simply said, *"Ground-Concepts"* [*Grundbegriffe*] means for us here: grasping [*begreifen*] the ground of beings as a whole. To grasp, however, does not mean that we merely permit ourselves to represent the ground and to have thoughts about it. When we have grasped something we also say something has opened up to us. This means for the most part that we have been transported into what has opened up and remain determined by it from now on. Thus "to grasp" [*Be-greifen*] the ground means above all that the "essence" of the ground embraces us into itself [*ein-begriffen*], and that it speaks to us in our knowing about it. *Grasping* announces itself to us as *being-embraced-into the "essence" of the ground.* This being-embraced-into does not consist exclusively in a "knowing," although it has the essential characteristic of a knowing. This knowing, however, can remain concealed from itself for a long time, and can block the way to itself. Nevertheless, even so veiled, this knowing permeates the history of mankind and is the bedrock in the mountain range of history. Man does not occasion this knowing of the ground through mere flashes of insight, nor can he force it through the art of mere cleverness. What he can do, and constantly does in one way or another, is only to remain within this knowing or forget it, to become aware of it (remembrance) or evade it.

PART ONE

Considering the Saying
The Difference between Beings and Being

FIRST DIVISION

Discussion of the "Is," of Beings as a Whole

§ *2. Beings as a whole are actual, possible, necessary*

Let us follow the ancient saying:

μελέτα τὸ πᾶν

"Take into care beings as a whole." And if we attempt to think the whole of beings at once, then we think, roughly enough, this: *that* the whole of beings "is," and we consider *what* it "is." We think the whole of beings, everything that is, in its being. In so doing we think at first something indeterminate and fleeting, and yet we also mean something for which we find nothing comparable, something singular. For the whole of beings does not occur twice, otherwise it wouldn't be what we mean.

To what "is" belongs not only the currently actual, which affects us and which we stumble upon: the happenings, the destinies and doings of man, nature in its regularity and its catastrophes, the barely fathomable powers that are already present in all motives and aims, in all valuations and attitudes of belief. To what "is" belongs also the possible, which we expect, hope for, and fear, which we only anticipate, before which we recoil and yet do not let go. To be sure, the possible is the not yet actual, but this not-actual is nevertheless no mere nullity. The possible also "is," its being simply has another character than the actual.

Different yet again from what happens to be actual and the possible is the necessary. Thus beings do not exhaust themselves in the actual. To beings belong the wealth of the possible and the stringency of the necessary. The realm of beings is not identical to the domain of the actual.

In terms of number, but above all in terms of modality, we mean more than the "actual" when we say "beings." Indeed, the actual is perhaps not at all the standard for beings. And whenever one demands closeness to the actual for human life, the "actuality" that is really meant is not what is simply present, but what is planned, not what is mastered, but an unspoken claim to power. The oft-mentioned "actual" is not the actual, but the possible. Thus we never think "beings" as a whole as long as we only mean the actual. Henceforth, if we earnestly think beings *as a whole,* if we think their being completely, then the actuality of the actual is contained in being, but also the possibility of the possible and the necessity of the necessary.

It remains to be asked why precisely these three (possibility, actuality, necessity) belong to being, whether they alone exhaust its essence. For metaphysics (ontology) it is clearly decided, beforehand and without any consideration, that these three types of beings, also simply called "the" "modalities" (actuality, possibility, necessity), exhaust the essence of being. That a being is either actual, possible, or necessary strikes ordinary understanding as a truism. However, this is perhaps a misunderstanding of the other truism that beings are actual and the actual is the effective and what counts at any particular time.

§3. Nonconsideration of the essential distinction between being and beings

But what passes itself off as even more self-evident is just that beings "are," or, as we say, are determined "by being." When we say "beings are," we distinguish each time between beings and their being, without noticing this distinction at all. Thus we also do not ask what this distinction consists in, from whence it originates, how it remains so obvious, and where it gets the right to this obviousness. We also do not find the slightest reason to concern ourselves with this distinction between being and beings in the first place.

When we consider the whole of beings, or even just attempt to think about it in a vague way, we leave what we envisage for the most part indeterminate and indistinct, whether beings or being, or both of them alternately and indefinitely, or each separately but in a barely comprehended relation. From here originates an old confusion of speech. We say "being" and really mean beings. We talk about beings as such and mean, at bottom, being. The distinction between beings and being seems not to obtain at all. If it does obtain, ignoring it seems not to cause any particular "harm."

Things take their course. However, we do not first hold ourselves within the above-mentioned distinction between beings and being when we reflect upon the whole of beings and actually consider its being. The distinction pervades all of our speaking about beings, indeed, it pervades every comportment toward beings whatever they might be, whether toward beings that we ourselves are not (stone, plant, animal) or beings that we ourselves are.

When we say, for example, completely outside scientific deliberation and far from all philosophical contemplation, "the weather is fine," and then by "weather" we mean something actual and existing, and we mean with "fine" the actual condition, and we mean with the inconspicuous "is" the manner in which this being, the weather, thus and so exists. Hence we mean the being of the being that is called "weather." The "is" does not thereby name a being, unlike "the weather" and "fine." Conversely, "the weather" and "fine" name a being, unlike the "is."

The weather is determined by the warmth of the sun, by the radiation of the earth and by its soil conditions, by wind (air current), by relative humidity, by the electrical conditions of the atmosphere, and more of the same. We can directly observe and, with the appropriate apparatus, assess the weather and what is relevant to it. We can decide if the weather is *good* or *bad* or *"doubtful."* What is good or bad or doubtful about the weather, we can see, sense. We can encounter the weather and its condition. But wherein lies the "is"? What does it mean, what does it consist in, that the weather "is" and that it "is" fine? The fine weather—that we can be glad about, but the "is"? What are we to make of it? We can read from the hygrometer whether the air is more or less humid, but there are no instruments to measure and comprehend the "is" of what we mean by "is." Thus we say with complete clumsiness: there are hygrometers, wind gauges, barometers that indicate how the weather "is," but there are no "is"-gauges, no instrument that could measure and take hold of the "is." And yet we say the weather—itself, namely,—is thus and so. We always mean by this what a being is, whether it is, and the way it "is." We mean the being of beings. While we mean something like this, namely being, we nevertheless attend only to particular beings.

In the case above we are interested only in the weather conditions, only in the weather, but not in the "is." How many times a day do we use this inconspicuous word "is," and not only in relation to the weather? But what would come of our taking care of daily business if each time, or even only one time, we were to genuinely think of the "is" and allow ourselves to linger over it, instead of immediately and exclusively involving ourselves with the respective beings that affect our intentions, our work, our amusements, our hopes and fears? We are familiar with *what* is, beings themselves, and we experience *that* they are. But the "is"—where in all the world are we supposed to find it, where are we supposed to look for something like this in the first place?

§4. The nondiscoverability of the "is"

"The leaf is green." We find the green of the leaf in the leaf itself. But where is the "is"? We say, nevertheless, the leaf "is"—it itself, the leaf. Consequently the "is" must belong to the visible leaf itself. But we do not "see" the "is" in the leaf, for it would have to be colored or spatially formed. Where and what "is" the "is"?

The question remains strange enough. It seems to lead to an empty hairsplitting, a hairsplitting about something that does not and need not trouble us. The cultivation of fruit trees takes its course without thinking about the "is," and botany acquires information about the leaves of plants without otherwise knowing anything else about the "is." It is enough that beings are. Let's stay with beings; wanting to think about the "is" "is" mere quibbling. Or instead we intentionally steer clear of a simple answer to the question as to where the "is" can be found.

Let's stay with the last example. "The leaf is green." Here we shall take "the green leaf itself," the designated being, as the "object." Now, insofar as the "is" is not discoverable in this object, it must belong to the "subject," that means to the person who judges and asserts propositions. Each person can be regarded as a "subject" in relation to the "objects" that they encounter. But how does it stand with the subjects, of whom each can say "I" about itself, of whom many can say "we" about themselves? These "subjects" also "are" and must "be." To say that the "is" in the proposition "the leaf is green" lies in the "subject" is only to defer the question. For the "subject" is also a "being," and thus the same question repeats itself. Indeed, it is perhaps still more difficult to say just to what extent "being" belongs to the subject, and belongs to it such that it would be transferred from here, so to speak, to "objects." In addition, when we understand the green leaf as an "object," we grasp it immediately and only in its relation to the subject, and precisely not as an independent being that we address in the "is" and "is green" in order to articulate what pertains to the being itself.

The flight from object to subject is in many respects a questionable way out. Thus we must reach still further and take notice for the first time of what we mean by the "is."

§5. The unquestioned character of the "is" in its grammatical determination—emptiness and richness of meaning

When we take the "is" as a "word" we label it, according to grammar, as a derivation and form of the verb "to be." We can also elevate this "verb" into a noun: being. We can easily take notice of this grammatically determinable derivation, but it contributes nothing to our understanding of what is named by the words "to be," "being," "is," "are," "was," "shall be," "has been." Finally we shall find out that no special assistance is needed in order to understand these words.

We say "the weather is fine." We can ask whether it really is fine, and whether it will last or isn't already starting to change. There can be doubt as to the characteristics of this being—the weather—but not about the "is," that is to say, not about what the "is" means here. Also when it becomes questionable if the weather is "good" or "bad," and we ask "Is the weather really as bad as it looks from this corner?"—then the "is" itself remains entirely unquestioned in the question. There is nothing questionable about the "is"—about what we mean by it. But how is it supposed to become questionable? For indeed in the word "is" something is thought that has no special content, no determination. "The weather is fine," "the window is closed," "the street is dark," here we constantly meet with the same empty meaning. The fullness and variability of beings never comes from the "is" and from being, but from beings themselves: weather, window, street, bad, closed, dark. When we say about beings that they are thus and so, we might distinguish between beings and being. But in this distinction being and the "is" remains continually indifferent and uniform, for it is emptiness itself. Indeed, perhaps we fall into a trap, so to speak, and attach to a linguistic form questions that have no support in what is actual. Useless hairsplitting instead of investigating the actual!?

Suppose we say, to stay with the weather, "it rains." Here the "is" does not present itself at all, and yet we mean that something actually "is." But what is the point of all this fuss over the empty little word "is"? The indeterminacy and emptiness of the word "is" is not eliminated by putting a noun in place of the "is" and pronouncing the name "being." At best, it is even increased.

It could appear that something important is concealed in what is named by the noun "being," something important and in this case especially profound, even though the title "being" nevertheless remains just a nametag for emptiness.

And yet, behind the uniformity and emptiness of the word "is," a scarcely considered richness conceals itself. We say: "this man is from

Swabia"; "the book is yours"; "the enemy is in retreat"; "red is port"; "God is"; "there is a flood in China"; "the goblet is silver"; "the soldier is on the battlefield"; "the potato beetle is in the fields"; "the lecture is in room 5"; "the dog is in the garden"; "this man is the devil's own." "Above all summits/Is rest. . . . "

Each time, the "is" has a different meaning and import for speech. We do not want to avoid this complexity but rather to emphasize it, for such a survey of the obvious can serve as a preliminary exercise for something else.

"The man is from Swabia" says: he originates from there; "the book is yours" says: it belongs to you; "the enemy is in retreat" means: he has begun to withdraw; "red is port" means: the red color is a sign for . . . ; "God is" is supposed to mean: God exists, he is actually there; "there is a flood in China" means: there something prevails, spreads, and results in destruction; "the goblet is silver" means: according to its material characteristics, it consists of . . . ; "the soldier is on the battlefield" would say: he engages the enemy; "the potato beetle is in the fields" establishes that: this animal causes damage there; "the lecture is in room 5" means: the lecture takes place there; "the dog is in the garden" means to say: the dog is located there, runs around there; "this man is the devil's own" means: he acts as if possessed by evil. "Above all summits/Is rest . . . " means— yes, what does this mean? Above all summits "rest locates itself"? Or: "takes place"? "exists"? "spreads"?—"Above all summits/Is rest."— Here not one of the above-mentioned elucidations of the "is" fits. And when we collect them together and add them up, their sum does not suffice either. Indeed, no paraphrase at all will do, so we simply have to leave the "is" to itself. And thus the same "is" remains, but simple and irreplaceable at once, the same "is" enunciated in those few words that Goethe wrote upon the mullions in a hut on the Kickelhahn at Ilmenau (cf. the letter to Zelter of Sept. 4, 1831).

How strange, that in response to Goethe's word "Above all summits/Is rest" we vacillate over an attempted elucidation of the familiar "is," and hesitate to give any elucidation at all, so that we come to give up completely and only say the same words over and again: "Above all summits/ Is rest." We forgo an elucidation of the "is," not because its understanding could be too complicated, too difficult, even hopeless, but because here the "is" is said as if for the first and only time. This is something so unique and simple that we don't have to do anything on our part to be addressed by it. Hence the "intelligibility" of the "is" that precludes all elucidation, the "intelligibility" that has perhaps a completely different mode than that familiarity in which the "is" otherwise occurs to us, constantly unthought, in everyday discourse.

All the same, the simple "is" of Goethe's poem holds itself far away from the mere indeterminacy and emptiness that we indeed easily master, if only through the hastiness of our understanding. Here, on the contrary, and despite its intelligibility, we are not at all equal to the address of this word, but are admitted into something inexhaustible.

"Above all summits/Is rest . . . "; in this "is" speaks the uniqueness of a gathered wealth. Not the emptiness of the indeterminate, but the fullness of the overdetermined prevents an immediate delimitation and interpretation of the "is." The insignificant word "is" thus begins to shine brightly. And the hasty judgment about the insignificance of the "is" starts to waver.

We now recognize the wealth of what the "is" has to say and is capable of saying, only in different respects from the complexity of the enumerated propositions. If we attempt to transfer the meaning of the "is" from any one of the above-cited propositions to the others, we immediately fail. Thus the emptiness and uniformity of the "is" shows itself to be a clumsy pretense that clings to the sameness of the sounds and the written characters. But how, then, is the alleged wealth supposed to lie in the "is" itself?

The word "is," taken by itself, remains helpless and poor in meaning. Why it is so with the "is," indeed why it must be so, is also easy to see. The complexity of the meanings of the "is" has its intelligible ground in the fact that a different being is represented each time in the above-cited propositions: the man from Swabia, the book, the enemy, the color red, God, the flood, the goblet, the soldier, the potato beetle, the lecture, the dog, the evil man, and finally in Goethe's poem—what? "Rest"? Is "rest" represented there and something about it ascertained, that it is present "above all summits"?

Here again, we hesitate over the interpretation. And that is no wonder, since the propositions cited above are "prosaic" observations and declarations, while in the last example precisely a "poetic" proposition was brought forward. In "poetic propositions," if they may be called "propositions" at all, things do not lie on the surface as much as they do in familiar, everyday discourse. The "poetic" is the exception. The rule and the ordinary are not to be gathered from it, and that means whatever can be discerned of the "is" commonly and in general. Therefore we may hope to ascend to the level of "higher," "poetic" expression, and to be able to attempt its clarification, only when the meaning of the "is" is first clarified satisfactorily in the common assertive proposition. Thus it is perhaps just as well that we do not allow ourselves to be prematurely confused by the "poetic" example that was merely tacked on to the end of the propositional sequence.

The previously cited propositions suffice, then, to demonstrate that the "is" derives its meaning each time from the being that is respectively represented, addressed, and articulated in the proposition. Only thus can it fill the emptiness that is otherwise, and indeed characteristically, inherent in it from case to case, and present itself in the appearance of a fulfilled word.

a) The emptiness and indeterminacy of the "is" as a presupposition for its being a "copula"

Citing the examples above thus proves the exact opposite of what is supposed to be shown, not a richness of the "is" but precisely its emptiness. Hence the impression afforded at first by this much-used word is confirmed, i.e., that of an indeterminate and not further determinable word, which is the essential mode of this word. Indeed, the alleged emptiness of this word, the "is," can be properly demonstrated as soon as we cease to deal with it in an approximate way. Let us attend to the character of this word instead of the many examples of its application, which can easily be multiplied to infinity. Grammar informs us about this. According to grammar, the "is" has the task of connecting the "subject" with the "predicate." The "is" is therefore called the "link" or "copula."

The connecting remains dependent upon what is supposed to be connected, and the mode of the bond is determined by the mode of what is supposed to come into connection. That the "is" has the character of the copula shows clearly enough the extent to which its meaning must be characterized by emptiness and indeterminacy. For only thus can the "is" suffice for the various uses that are constantly demanded of it in discourse. The "is" remains not only actually an empty word, but due to its essence—as a connecting word—it may not be loaded down beforehand with any particular meaning. Its own meaning must therefore be totally "empty."

b) Being ("is") as the general, the universal

The uniformity of the "is" therefore cannot be passed off as a mere appearance. It distinguishes this word and thus indicates that the noun "being," derived from its infinitive "to be," also only signifies a perhaps indispensable but fundamentally empty representation. This uniformity is won by turning our view from beings and their respective determinations and retaining only the empty universal. For a long time now "being" has therefore been called the most common, the "general," the most general of all that is general. In this word, and in what it means, the solidity of each respective being evaporates into the haziest haze of the most universal. Hence Nietzsche calls "being" the "last breath of a vaporizing reality."

If, however, being thus vaporizes and disappears, what becomes of the difference between being and beings?

In this difference, we "have" before us two differentia: beings and being. If, however, one of the two differentia in this difference, namely being, is only the emptiest universalization of the other, owes its essence to the other, and if consequently everything that has content and endures shifts to the side of beings, and being is in truth nothing, or at best an empty word-sound, then the differentiation may not be taken as completely valid. For it to be valid, each of the two "sides" would have to be able to maintain a genuine and radical claim to essence from out of itself.

If we are to consider the whole of beings, then we could certainly give the most universal but also the emptiest of beings the name "being." But we fall at once into error when, fooled by the naming and establishing of the name "being," we chase after a so-called "being itself" instead of considering only beings (is . . . to be—being—being itself). Indeed, we do not simply fall once more into error, but into the mere emptiness of the purely null, where inquiry no longer finds any support, where there is nothing to be in error about. If we want to follow the saying μελέτα τὸ πᾶν, we therefore do well to avoid the phantom of an "abstract concept" named by the word "being."

§6. The solution of healthy common sense: Acting and effecting among beings instead of empty thinking about being (workers and soldiers)

But an alert sense for the actual and a healthy instinct for "realities" do not need such far-ranging reflections. These are already abstract enough, and additionally, they attempt to demonstrate the emptiness and ground-lessness of the abstract. A forthright man experiences the whole of beings not through the dislocations of empty thinking about "being" but only by acting and effecting among beings. Of course, not every random activity guarantees a coalescence with the actual, and thus "the concrete," in distinction from the abstract. For this, participation in the inner law of the age is needed. But where this participation occurs, there awakens a heightened knowledge which is delivered over to something necessary, and that means indispensable for it. Therein lies an authentic concept of being free and freedom articulated by Nietzsche (see *Twilight of the Idols,* 1888).

But who would deny that active participation in the actual takes place in various levels of knowing and acting, and must do so completely for an age in which the "Will to Power" alone everywhere determines the fundamental characteristic of acting, and even rules over the most apparently opposed standpoints, so that nothing more remains of the previous world? Who would deny that here all human planning and effecting displays, in particular clarity, the character of a great "game," in which no individual nor even everyone together can muster the stakes at risk in this "world-play"? Who could wonder that in such a time, when the world as we have known it is coming out of joint, the thought arises that now only the love of danger and "adventure" can be the way man secures the actual for himself?

Nietzsche says: " . . . every higher man feels himself to be *an adventurer.*"[2] In any case, it becomes clear that all interpretations of humanity and its determination, issuing from previous explanations of the world, lag behind what is. In the meantime, it has been decided that *"the worker"* and *"the soldier"* completely determine the face of the actual, all political systems in the narrow sense notwithstanding. These names are not meant here as names for a social class or profession. They indicate, in a unique fusion, the type of humanity taken as measure by the present world-convulsion for its fulfillment, that gives direction and foundation to one's relation to beings. The names "worker" and "soldier" are thus metaphysical titles and name that form of the human fulfillment of the being of beings, now become manifest, which Nietzsche presciently grasped as the *"will to power."*

This emerging formation of humanity was already clear to Nietzsche in the eighties of the last century, not from observations of social and political conditions, but from metaphysical knowledge about the self-fulfilling and long-decided essential form of being as will to power.

Three sketches from the decade between 1880 and 1890 might suffice to prove this. We must forgo a more exact interpretation here.

In 1882 Nietzsche writes (*Will to Power,* 764): "The workers shall live one day as the bourgeoisie do now—but above them, distinguished by their freedom from wants, the *higher caste:* thus poorer and simpler, but in possession of power."

In 1885/86 Nietzsche writes (*Will to Power,* 757): "Modern socialism wants to create the secular counterpart to Jesuitism: *everyone* a perfect instrument. But the purpose, the wherefore? has not yet been found."

In November 1887/March 1888 Nietzsche writes (*Will to Power,* 763):

---

2. F. Nietzsche, *Nachgelassene Werke, Unveröffentlichtes aus der Umwertungszeit* (1882/32–1888); *Nietzsches Werke,* part 2, vol. XII (Leipzig, 1903), p. 54, no. 128.

"*From the future of the worker*—workers should learn to feel like soldiers. An honorarium, an income, but no pay!

"No relation between payment and *achievement!* But to place the individual, *each according to his kind,* so that he can *achieve the highest* that lies within his realm."[3]

In these sketches by Nietzsche the names "worker," "soldier," and "socialism" are already titles for the leading representatives of the main forms in which the will to power will be enacted!

"Workers" and "soldiers" open the gates to the actual. At the same time, they execute a transformation of human production in its basic structure; of what formerly was called "culture." The latter, according to previous notions, is an instrument of "cultural politics." Culture only exists insofar as it is plugged into [*eingeschaltet*] the operations that secure a basis for a form of domination. That we use the term "plug in" [*einschalten*] to name this connection, an expression from machine technology and machine utilization, is like an automatic proof of the actuality that finds words here. "Workers" and "soldiers" remain obviously conventional names that nevertheless can signify, roughly and in outline, the humanity now arising upon the earth. If the peasant transforms himself into a worker in the provisions industry, then this is the same process by which a leading scholar becomes the managing director of a research institute. But it would be backward and only half serious, thus not at all seriously thought out, to try to characterize these events in terms of past "political" ideas, e.g., as a "proletarianization," and to believe thereby that we had grasped the slightest thing. To interpret everything from what has been, and thus to exclude oneself from the realm of the already actual and its essential being, corresponds to natural human inertia. Only a dreamer and a visionary could want to deny that, in the age dawning upon the entire earth, man experiences real beings as a worker and soldier does, and makes available what alone is to count as a being.

Only those who are permanently ill-tempered and angry on principle

3. F. Nietzsche, *Nachgelassene Werke*, vol. XVI: *Der Wille zur Macht. Versuch einer Umwertung aller Werte*, Books 3 and 4 (Leipzig, 1911). English translation: *The Will to Power*, trans. Walter Kaufmann and R. J. Hollingdale (New York: Vintage, 1968).

could propose to stay essential decisions by flight into what has been, to whose past formation and preservation they have contributed nothing. Yet, genuine participation in the law of the age is also essentially other than the comportment that exhausts itself in advocating "optimism." For mere optimism is only a concealed pessimism, a pessimism that avoids itself. In this age of the convulsion of the entire world pessimism and optimism remain, in the same way, powerless for what is necessary. The sobriety of knowing and reflection upon what *is* are necessary above all. However, this sobriety includes recognizing the truth under which the history of the age stands. Sobriety also includes asking whether the uniqueness of this world-age demands of Dasein an originality for which having intellectual interests and attending to so-called cultural concerns, in addition to the life of action, do not suffice. For the genuine passion of sobriety the best optimism is too lame, every pessimism too blind. All this should indicate that the call to participate in the actual always stands under a different law; it does not each time guarantee a straightforward experience of what is. Certainly, today, "workers" and "soldiers" experience beings in helping to bring about their characteristic features.

§7. *Renouncing being—dealing with beings*

But do "workers" and "soldiers," in virtue of this experience, also know the being of beings? No. Yet perhaps they no longer need to know it. Perhaps the being of beings has never been experienced by those who directly shape, produce, and represent beings. Perhaps being was always brought to knowledge merely "by the way," like something apparently "superfluous."

If it were so, then within the realm of historical humanity, besides the boundless complexity and fullness of beings, this "superfluity," being, would still reveal itself. Then it would remain to ask whether this "super-fluity" is also the gift of a surplus and a wealth, or whether it always remains merely useless, the poverty of emptiness—the emptiness that already announced itself to us distinctly enough in the connecting word "is."

Without noticing it, we are again considering the difference between beings and being. Perhaps being cannot be so conveniently shoved aside, as the discussion of the copula seems to have succeeded in doing. Even when it is established that man knows nothing of being in all his experiences and dealings with beings, indeed that he needs to know nothing of being, then it is still by no means decided whether what he experiences before all beings, experiences differently and more originarily than any particular being, is what we call being. The remark that the word "is" means only an empty representation of something indeterminate and not further determinable can no longer suffice to decide what being "is" apart from beings.

Meanwhile, we have only given voice to the undeniable "fact" that the immediate experience of beings holds beings secure and therein finds contentment. One finds proof of "actuality" in the actual itself, equates the one (the actual) with the other (actuality), and, in case one still concedes a proper essence to "actuality," it is in the role of capturing the "universal representation" of the most universal—called being—in a word's sound. One is content with beings, and renounces being so decisively that one does not allow this renunciation to count as such, but declares it to be a gain: the advantage, from now on, of not being disturbed by the "abstract" in dealing with beings. Where does this remarkable contentment come from?

Perhaps this complacency about the experience and cultivation of beings stems from the fact that man, in the midst of beings, thinks only about what he needs. Why should he need a discussion of the meaning of the word "is"? Indeed—it is of no use. Discussions about the "is" in the proposition therefore also remain useless, even if it should turn out that we are not dealing with mere words and mere verbal meanings. This reflection is devoted to something superfluous and perhaps even to an excess.

For this reason alone, we do not prematurely cast aside discussions of the "is" in the proposition. Perhaps something essential conceals itself here, especially if everything essential occurs "despite" all that is nonessential. Everything decisive is "despite" the ordinary, for the ordinary and usual recognizes and wants only its own kind.

Perhaps the previous discussion of the "is," where the "is" is under-stood as the copula, was only an ordinary discussion, made ordinary by our long being accustomed to thinking of so-called "grammar" as appro-priate for imparting authoritative information about language and the word. Perhaps the ordinary must first of all be shaken, so that we receive a first sense of the superfluous. Thus, forsaking the beaten path of former opinion, we wish to take up anew the discussion of the "is" and "being."

Recapitulation

1. Consideration of beings as a whole presupposes the essential inclusion of man in the difference between being and beings

We follow an ancient saying, and in so doing cast off the hasty pre-sumption of a willful cleverness that would perhaps like merely to con-trive a worldview or "represent" a particular standpoint. This saying goes:

μελέτα τὸ πᾶν

"Take into care beings as a whole."

This saying in no way serves as a timeless rule, but demands that we follow it by returning to the inception to which it belongs, and that we experience in the incipient a unique decision. Accordance with this deci-sion does not mean imitating and renewing something earlier, but begin-ning something yet to come. *To follow the saying* means, at the same time and at once: *remembering what is incipient and deciding what is yet to come.* All this implies that we must single out Greek thought as a first begin-ning, but we can never prescribe it, as the "Classical," as a rule for ourselves.

Following the saying, we consider beings as a whole and see ourselves forced to acknowledge the possible and the necessary as beings. We must therefore give up the seductive identification of beings with the merely actual. The actual, to be sure, retains its priority in our experiences, opin-ions, and plans. But this priority does not necessarily entail the preemi-nence of the actual within the whole of beings. However, when we experience this whole in terms of its possibilities and necessities, beyond the merely actual, it remains to be decided whether we have indeed already traversed its domain.

Meanwhile, we have noticed that in thinking beings we also "thereby" think *being*. The whole of beings is neither merely the sum of all beings nor is it already thought when we succeed in representing its "totality." For if totality is not simply adventitious to the whole, but projects ahead of all beings as their determination (because it resonates through the whole of beings as "a being"), then totality itself is only a satellite of what distinguishes beings as beings. We call this "being." In considering beings as a whole we think the whole as a being, and thus we already think it from being. We differentiate each time, without knowing how or why or wherefore, beings and being.

Obviously we do not first make this differentiation and carry it with us like a piece of information, like an arbitrary differentiation such as that between red and green. Rather, we move within this differentiation of beings and being just as we stay, in advance, within the difference between right and left, where the differentia are of the same kind and concern a particular realm of the spatial.

If we need evidence that we always remain and encounter ourselves within this differentiation of beings and being, it suffices to note that we continually name being in our comportment toward beings when we say "is." Whether we actually assert propositions that contain this word "is" or silently busy and concern ourselves with beings is all the same. That we must continually say "is" whenever we speak indicates that what we "so" name, precisely being, wants to be put into a word, into a word that, admittedly, we always at the same time mis-hear. This failure to recognize the "is" resembles the all too familiar and monotonous tick of the clock within the usual sphere of everyday residing. We first hear the motion of the clock when it stands still. In just this way, we become aware of the "is" and what it says when an interruption intrudes upon speaking. To be sure, "we" can experience this interruption only hypothetically, only as possible, never as actual. We can posit the case where we utterly fail to say or even merely think the "is." What would happen then, each may work out at first for himself. It suffices simply to consider "externally" any series of utterances whatsoever in which we directly and continually say the insignificant word "is."

We consider beings as a whole, and thereby think being. Thus, in thinking, we move within the differentiation between beings and being. Not that we apply this differentiation and refer to it like a familiar rule. We are in accordance with it without actually knowing of it or having a concept of its essence and essential ground. Perhaps it is already too much and inappropriate when we speak of *the* differentiation between beings and being in the first place. For in this way a difference is already objectified without our being able to specify where it belongs, whether it only subsists because we carry it out, or whether man carries it out because something essential determines him—to which we want to cling fast, so to speak, under the empty name of the differentiation between beings and being. For otherwise many things are differentiated. What all isn't distinguishable and addressed as a differentiation! Talk of *the* differentiation is supposed to indicate, however, that this differentiation is the origin of all differences.

The differentiation / "beings and being" / contains an indication that after all "being" and "beings" harbor within themselves the relation *to* being. How exclusively we refer to being in every attitude toward beings is evidenced by our saying "is."

2. Wealth and poverty of meaning in the "is"

A survey of the quoted propositions made clear that the "is" in a proposition means something complex. A short pause at Goethe's verse "Above all summits/Is rest" showed beyond this that the "is" announces, in all simplicity, the inexhaustibility of a wealth to which we are not immediately equal.

The noun and name "being" names what we mean by the "is." In the wealth of meaning in the "is," the essential fullness of being shows itself. But when we look closely, it appears as if the "is" does not derive its complexity of meaning from the fullness of being, but always only from the fact that each time a different being, man, color, dog, etc., is named. Taken by itself, the "is," in fact, remains empty. Indeed, it must be empty according to its essence, like the word for the empty and indeterminate itself. For the "is" has the verbal character of the "copula" in the proposition. As this "connection," it must for its part be unbound and leave everything open and indeterminate, in order to be able to conjoin completely different beings. Thus the opposite of the previous conclusion shows itself: the "is" does not distinguish itself through fullness of meaning, but through poverty of meaning. The same holds even more, and even more properly, for the noun and name "being." Here emptiness and indeterminacy are made into a fetish. It looks as though being is not only "something" next to beings, but being and what constitutes the being of beings is the *most real being*. Thus already at the beginning of metaphysics Plato conceived the being of beings as the authentic being of all beings (ὄντως ὄν). By contrast, at the end of Western metaphysics, and that means *Platonism*, Nietzsche recognized being not as the most real but as the most negative. Nietzsche grasped being as the last breath of a vaporizing reality.

This contradictory interpretation of the being of beings, according to which being "is" first the most real and then the utmost nullity, shows two contrary versions of being. And yet it is a matter of the same interpretation. Its self-sameness is articulated in a fundamental doctrine of Western metaphysics. According to this, being is the *most universal of the universal* (κοινότατον). The most universal, which does not permit anything more universal for its determination, is the most indeterminate and emptiest. If it is so with being, then one side of the differentiation, that of being, loses weight against the other, that of beings. The one side becomes superfluous and there is no longer a distinction to be made.

3. Equating dealing with the actual with considering beings as a whole

If we are now still supposed to follow the saying and consider beings as a whole, then the task is clear and the direction is firm: we can and must cling to beings. "Take into care beings as a whole" now has a univocal sense, which suggests itself on its own and does not require any special reflection: stick to facts, deal with the actual and its actualization, and secure its effectiveness. Equating dealing with the actual with considering beings as a whole completely loses all questionability when we recognize, at the same time, that the correct recognition indeed lies only in such dealings. Acting and effecting bring to experience what the actual is, and thus what beings themselves are. Acting, however, is always accompanied by the *freedom* from whence man comports himself toward beings. Freedom is now participation in the law of the age. Nietzsche expressed its more determinate essence in the passage cited from *Twilight of the Idols:*

> For what is freedom? That one has the will to self-responsibility.[4]

This answer of Nietzsche's sounds like Kant's answer to the same question. Freedom is self-legislation, is placing oneself under the law of the self.

Nietzsche's answer not only sounds Kantian, it also thinks (in the essential sense) in a Kantian, i.e., modern, way. And yet Nietzsche thinks differently than Kant. For everything depends upon what the "self" means here, whose self-responsibility we are talking about. Being as self is the essence of the "subject." In distinction from but in internal connection with Kant, Nietzsche conceives being a self as the *will to power.* Freedom as will to self-responsibility then means: freedom as will to fulfill the "will to power." However, since according to Nietzsche the will to power is not only the being of "man," but also the being of atoms no less than the being of animals, since it is no less the essence of the political than the essence of art, *freedom as the will to the will to power* means the same as participation in the actuality of the actual.

4. The unthought residence of man in *the* distinction between being and beings

We reflect upon what the ancient saying "μελέτα τὸ πᾶν" says: "Take into care beings as a whole." The reflection leads us to recognize

---

4. F. Nietzsche, *Nachgelassene Werke,* part 1, vol. VIII (Leipzig, 1899), p. 149, no. 38.

something that until now we either did not realize at all or ignored, namely, that we think "being" everywhere and always, wherever and whenever in the midst of beings we comport ourselves toward beings, and are thereby beings ourselves, and thus comport ourselves toward ourselves at the same time. Briefly: we have our residence in *the* distinction between beings and being.

This domain of residence appears to us at first like something negative when we consider that the home ground, the place of a people and similar narrower or wider horizons, finally the earth itself, actually bear our residing and grant all comportment toward beings its expanse. But what would all of this, home and earth, be, if it did not reveal itself to us *as* beings, if beings as such and therefore beings in their mode of being did not permeate and charge our attunement? That the distinction between beings and being looks to us (and that means to our ordinary, superficial opining and hurried "thinking") like something indifferent and negative is indeed not sufficient evidence that this distinction could not perhaps be something entirely different in its essence, whose dignity we could never overestimate, but rather, at best, and to our own detriment, we must always underestimate.

This distinction between beings and being holds the differentia apart from one another, and this apartness is in itself an extension and an expanse that we must recognize as the space of all spaces—so far as we may still use this name "space" at all here, which indeed means only a particular type of apartness.

At first, certainly, we know nothing of this distinction. What it consists in remains hidden. Whether what constitutes its essence is at all characterized by means of the code word "distinction" remains undecided, indeed, unasked. For "distinction" is many things. Distinction is, for example, everything opposed to something that we encounter among beings. Metaphysics also finds opposition and distinction within being and its essence (cf. German Idealism). What is here called *"the* distinction" between beings and being is more essential than all differences in beings and all oppositions in being.

SECOND DIVISION

Guidewords for Reflection upon Being

§8. Being is the emptiest and at the same time a surplus

Adhering to what was said before, when we consider afresh the "is" as the connecting word in a proposition we must already acknowledge two things. The "is" indicates an emptiness in which reflection finds no support. However, at the same time, the "is" divulges a wealth within which the being of beings pronounces itself.

Let us think again upon Goethe's verse, which, in terms of content, speaks only of "mountainpeaks" and "above" and "rest." And yet, the "is" names something that cannot be determined by what is named and nameable through this content. Thus precisely in the "is" a peculiar claim is spoken, which flows from its own source and cannot be exhausted or drained by the naming of various beings. Therefore the very slightness of the verse says much, indeed still "more" than an extended description.

In the "is" a surplus is put into words. If we replace the "is" with the name of the noun "being," then, if we consider what is said in its unity, we stand before the question: Is "being" only the emptiest, as measured against each being thus-and-thus determined? Or is being a surplus for all beings, which leaves each being infinitely far behind? Or is being perhaps yet both, the emptiest as well as the surplus? Being would then be, in its very essence, its own opposite. We would then have to acknowledge something like a discord within being itself.

If, however, this discordant character belongs to being itself, and constitutes its essential character, then being cannot be split in the sense of a destruction of its essence. What is discordant must then be held together in the unity of an essence. But we would be overhasty to speak directly about an essential discordance of being, and to presume to decide about the essence of being solely on the grounds of the double character of the "is" (that it announces itself at once as emptiness and surplus). Above all, we resist the temptation to take this emerging discordance within being as the occasion for a dialectical accounting of being, and thus to choke off all reflection. We want at first only to carry out a reflection, and so to clarify our relation to the being of beings. We concern ourselves with this clarification of our relation to the being of beings in order first to come into position to perceive, with a certain clarity, the claim of that saying: μελέτα τὸ πᾶν.

From the just-completed reflection, however, we first discern this about being: *Being is the emptiest and at the same time a surplus*, out of which all beings, those that are familiar and experienced as well as those unfamiliar and yet to be experienced, are granted their respective modes of being.

§9. Being is the most common and at the same time unique

If we follow this indication of being in all beings, we immediately find that being is encountered in every being uniformly and without difference. Being is common to all beings and thus is the most common.

The most common is without every distinction: the stone is, the tree is, the animal is, and man is, the "world" is, and God "is." Against this thoroughly "uniform" "is," and in contrast to this uniformity and leveling of being, many levels and ranks show themselves within beings, which themselves allow the most diverse arrangements. We can progress from the lifeless, from dust and sand and the motionlessness of stone, to the "living" of plants and animals, beyond this to free men, and yet beyond this to demigods and gods. We could also reverse the order of rank among beings and declare what one ordinarily calls "spirit" and the "spiritual" to be only a discharge of electrical phenomena and an excretion of materials whose composition, to be sure, chemistry has not yet discovered but will discover one day. Or, we can appoint those beings that we call "living" to the highest rank and hold "life" to be *the* actual and figure everything material into it, and incorporate into it the "spiritual" as well, solely as a tool for "life." Nevertheless, *being* is each time thoroughly common in all beings and thus the most common. At the same time, however, a cursory reflection just as soon encounters the opposite of this characterization of being. However one being might surpass another, *as* a being it remains equal to the other, hence it has in the other its own equivalent. Every being has in every being, insofar as it is a being, *its equal*. The tree in front of the house is a different being than the house, but a being; the house is other than a man, but a being. All beings are thrown into the manifoldness of respective beings, separated from one another, and dispersed into a vast multiplicity. In experiencing beings we pass through many kinds of things. And yet, *everywhere and without exception, beings find in each being their equal.* How does it stand, however, with being?

Being has its equal nowhere and nohow. Being is, over and against all beings, unique.

Nothing corresponds to being. Being is not given a second time. There are certainly different modes of being, but precisely *of* being, which is never respectively this and that and thus constantly a plurality like beings. The uniqueness of being has incomparability as a consequence. Beings can always be compared with beings and placed into equivalence with one another. However, being is never merely what is equivalent in the manifold beings stone, plant, animal, man, God. For to be what is equivalent it would have to be multiple. Being, by contrast, is everywhere *the same*, namely, itself. In order to be equivalent, something other and additional is required. To be the same, *only* uniqueness is needed. As the same and unique, being is, of course, forever different in and from itself. But what is differentiated is not different in the sense that being could be being twice over and repeatedly, and would be split and divided into multiplicity. Being is distinguished by uniqueness in a unique way, incomparable with any other distinction. Being in its *uniqueness*—and in addition to this, beings in their *multiplicity*.

But is there not a third thing, which we must distinguish in addition to being and beings—*the Nothing*?

One could cut off this question with the observation that the Nothing precisely is not, and therefore there is no sense or reason to speak of a third thing here. It is indeed correct that the Nothing is not a being and can never and nowhere be made into a being, for we think the Nothing as the negation of beings purely and simply. But the question remains whether the Nothing itself consists in the negation of beings, or whether the negation of beings is simply a representation of the Nothing, which the Nothing requires of us when we set out to think it. For the Nothing is certainly no being, but nevertheless "there is given" [*es gibt*] the Nothing. We say here "there is given" the Nothing, but we cannot, at present, determine more closely who or what gives the Nothing. We can also say the Nothing *presences* [*west*], in order to indicate that the Nothing is not merely the absence and lack of beings. If the Nothing were only something indifferently negative, how could we understand, for example, horror and terror before the Nothing and nihilation? Terror *before* the Nothing—.

The Nothing does not first need beings and a being in order to presence, as if it would presence only if beings were eliminated in advance. The Nothing is not the result of such an elimination. There is given the Nothing in spite of the fact that beings are. And perhaps it is one of the greatest of human errors to believe oneself always secure before the Nothing so long as beings can be encountered and dealt with and retained. Perhaps the predominance of this error is a main reason for blindness *vis-à-vis* the Nothing, which cannot affect beings, and least of all when beings become more and more "existant" [*seiender*]. Perhaps the belief that the Nothing is just "nothing" is also the main support for a popular piece of intelligence, namely: every reflection upon the Nothing leads to nothingness and endangers the legitimate trust in beings.

If, however, the Nothing is obviously not a being, we cannot at all say that it "is." Nevertheless, *"there is given"* the Nothing. We ask again: what does "there is given" mean here? What is given "is" yet somehow something. But the Nothing is not "something," jut nothing. Here we easily fall into the danger of playing with words. People make use of the justifiable indication of this danger in order to banish all thought "about" the Nothing as fatal. But the danger is no less that, because we seem to be merely playing around with words, we take the Nothing too lightly and fail to recognize that there is given the Nothing. If this should be the case, we would indeed have to say that the Nothing is. But if we say this we make the Nothing into a being and twist it into the opposite of itself. Or else the "is" we use when we say "the Nothing is" means something other than when we say "beings are." Perhaps we merely cling obstinately to an untested everyday assumption when we insist that the "is" is used in the same sense in the propositions "beings are" and "the Nothing is." A more penetrating reflection might make us suddenly realize that the Nothing does not need beings in order to be the Nothing as a result of their elimination.

The Nothing does not need beings. Certainly, however, the Nothing needs being. That the Nothing needs precisely being, and without being must remain without essence, remains strange and shocking to the ordinary understanding. Indeed, perhaps the Nothing is even the same as being. For the uniqueness of being can never be endangered by the Nothing, because the Nothing "is" not something other than being, but this itself. Does not what we said about being also hold for the Nothing: that it is unique and incomparable? The incontrovertible incomparability of the Nothing is evidence that its essence belongs to being and confirms being's uniqueness.

That the Nothing "is" the same as being, that the Nothing is related in its essence to being, if not essentially one with it, we can also surmise from what has already been said about being: "Being is the emptiest." Is the Nothing not the emptiest emptiness? The Nothing also shares uniqueness with being in this respect.

Hence we discern from our considerations so far: *Being is the emptiest and at the same time a surplus. Being is the most common of all and at the same time unique.*

What we say about being in such propositions, here and in what follows, cannot count as the sufficiently presented and demonstrated "truth" about being. Certainly, however, we take these propositions as *guidewords for the reflection upon being,* which we also think whenever and however we think back, in remembering, to the ancient saying.

§10. *Being is the most intelligible and at the same time concealment*

The very preliminary discussions of being in respect to the "is" in a proposition have already taught us that we understand the "is" and "being" everywhere and immediately. For this we do not need any special experiences and ratiocinations. The intelligibility of the "is" in a proposition remains for us so familiar and certain in advance that at first we pay no special attention to it at all. In addition, where we actually concern ourselves with the explanation of beings and must halt before an "unintelligible" being, where our investigations among beings find their limit, even there the unexplained being remains for us embedded within a circuit of the intelligible. This is evidenced for the most part in that we arrange the unintelligible being immediately within the intelligible, and most often in an already familiar fashion.

When, for instance, in respect to a domain of beings, e.g., nature, the confidence prevails that what is hitherto unexplained and unexplainable will yet be explained with time and in the course of human progress, behind this confidence already stands the procedure that assumes the intelligibility of being and beings. In our time we can easily give an especially impressive example of the limitless power of confidence in respect to the intelligibility of beings. (See the article by Pascual Jordan, "Am Rande der Welt."[5] The article is also a revealing example of the inner decadence of today's "science." Take especially the practical application at the conclusion! By contrast, take the serious and careful essay by C. F. v. Weizsäcker, "Die Physik der Gegenwart und das physikalische Weltbild."[6])

---

5. P. Jordan, "Am Rande der Welt: Betrachtungen zur modernen Physik," *Die neue Rundschau,* 52 (1941), 290–297.
6. D. F. v. Weizsäcker, "Die Physik der Gegenwart und das physikalische Weltbild," *Die Naturwissenschaften,* 29, vol. 13 (1941), 185–194.

In the realm of atomic processes, modern atomic and quantum physics have discovered events where the discharges observable in this realm as a "statistical average" do conform to certain rules, yet in particular are not "foreseeable." What is "unforeseeable," i.e., what cannot be computed in advance from within the purview of physical calculation, shows itself each time as something new and cannot be explained by something else. Whatever cannot be explained as a consequence of an antecedent other, *as* antecedent, lacks a cause. In the field of atomic physics, one says,the law of causality is invalid. This invalidity of the law of causality, one believes, is established in a purely physical way by research. However, one does not rest content with this allegedly enormous discovery, which, furthermore, serves to refute Kant and all previous philosophy. One applies the statement of the invalidity of the causal law in the atomic realm immediately to the "positive" realm. When something is "uncaused" by something else and is thus new, originating from itself, it is then "spontaneous," and if spontaneous, "free." One speaks therefore of the "peculiar" freedom of action belonging to the microphysical structure.

(The discharge of atomic processes is, to be sure, not "peculiar." Only the physics is "peculiar" which makes a thoughtless fool of itself with such assertions, and does not anticipate how it must betray its essential superficiality, the result of which is that it cannot decide anything "for" or "against" "causality.")

But with that, one might think physics has secured a domain for physical research in which the "living" and the "spiritual," and everything characterized by "freedom," fit in perfectly. Thus opens the "promising" vista that one day "human freedom" can also be proven by "natural science" to be a "natural-scientific fact." I am not relating fictional stories, nor reporting the fancies of a half-educated dreamer who patches together a "worldview" from "books" he has arbitrarily picked up. I am reporting the scientific conviction of today's physicists, who as researchers place the "exactness" of thought above everything, whose work is already confirmed by unforeseen technical success and presumably will continue to be confirmed in ways none of us anticipate. However, because mere success is never a proof of truth but is always the "consequence" of a grounding principle whose truth must first be questioned and which can never be decided by the continually dependent result, the success of today's "science" is no argument for its truth, and is not something that could keep us from asking a question.

What is happening here? What commonly occurs to one in representing the atomic realm, and what is taken as the fundamental determination of the being of the physical domain, is held to be the intellegible *per se*, and one arranges under it everything else. One speaks, without thinking, of "actions" and "freedom of action" in reference to atoms, and believes, therefore, one has penetrated into the domain of the organic. One already dreams of a "quantum biology" grounded by "quantum physics." How unquestioned these opinions of the researchers are is shown most clearly in that they believe themselves far superior to the so-called materialists with this type of research and approach. In contrast with the materialists, one grants validity to "freedom." However, one does not see that one equates freedom with physical unpredictability, and therefore physically pre-interprets everything human. Above all, one does not see that a privation lies in the determination of the unpredictable, and that this cannot be without the positivity of predictability, that means of causality. Causality is not overcome. On the contrary, it is confirmed to the utmost, only transformed, and, strictly speaking, ascertainable in the usual way.

One finds this procedure to be in order. For one is of the opinion that naturally everyone knows, off the street so to speak, what "freedom" and "spirit" and such things are, for one has and is these things oneself every day. Whereas, naturally, for example, an understanding of the mathematics of wave mechanics is accessible to only a very few mortals, and requires a Herculean effort and a corresponding technical preparation. But why should a physicist, who is also a human being, not know at the same time what is essential to human freedom and everything else that concerns man, and what can be discovered about it? Why shouldn't everyone be informed about all of this and about the being of beings in general? This attitude of the sciences, and these claims that we constantly encounter everywhere in modified forms, state unequivocally that for us the being of beings is the most intelligible thing of all. We do not remember ever having really learned what being "is" and means. To the contrary, we must indeed strive step by step for the cognizance of and acquaintance with particular beings. Whence stems as well the strange state of affairs wherein we require the highest exactitude for the study of beings, and above all, of "nature," and to that end set into motion gigantic apparatuses, whereas for the determination of being any arbitrary and approximate notion may and does suffice. That science, e.g., must put into operation complicated investigations in order historiologically to secure a historical fact is understandable. But it is no less understandable that any vague notions, wherever they may come from, are sufficient for judgments to be made and agreement to be found about the fundamental appearances of history, about human freedom, about the essence of power, about art, and about poetry. Respect for facts and for the exact determinations of beings must "naturally" be required. If, however, what is essential to beings, therefore to being, is abandoned to the claims of arbitrary notions, there is no occasion for reservations. All of this, and many similar things in human comportment, speak for the fact that being, as distinguished from beings, is the most intelligible. The intelligibility of being has, we do not know how and when, simply come our way.

However, when we are supposed to say expressly what we understand by such "most intelligible" being, and that means what we think with the word "being," and that means what we "grasp" being as, then we are suddenly at a loss. Suddenly it is shown to us that we not only have no concept for this most intelligible, for being, we also do not see how we are still supposed to grasp "something" here with respect to being. Within beings, the task and the way out remain for us to trace the given being back to another being that we take to be clearer and more familiar, and through this reduction to explain it, and to content ourselves with such an explanation. However, where it is a matter of grasping *being*, the way out by means of a being is denied to us if we earnestly stick to the question. For every being is, as such, already determined by being and lays claim to this for itself. Next to (*praeter*) any one being "are," to be sure, always various other beings, but besides being "there is given" at most the Nothing. Should we not, then, attempt to determine being from the Nothing?

However, the Nothing is itself the indeterminate *per se*. How should it offer something in terms of which we grasp being? This way, as well, leads

to no essential determination of being. Being thus denies itself every concept and every determination and illumination, and does so in every respect and for every attempt at an explanation. Being simply withholds itself from any grasping on the basis of beings. If we say that being simply withholds itself, then, yet again, we are saying something about being. This essence belongs to being: to withhold itself from explanation on the basis of beings. *Withholding itself*, it removes itself from determinacy, from manifestness. Withdrawing from manifestness, it conceals itself. *Self-concealment* belongs to being. If we wish to acknowledge this, then we must say: *Being itself "is" concealment.* Therefore, we must adhere to the following.
Being is the emptiest and at the same time a surplus.
Being is the most common of all and at the same time uniqueness.
Being is the most intelligible and at the same time concealment.

§11. Being is the most worn-out and at the same time the origin

If we now consider that being conceals itself, indeed that self-concealment belongs to being's essence, it might seem once again as if being remains completely and necessarily withdrawn from us. But again, it can only seem so. For we lay claim to being everywhere, wherever and whenever we experience beings, deal with them and interrogate them, or merely leave them alone. We need being because we need it in all relations to beings. In this constant and multiple use, being is in a certain way expended.

And yet we cannot say that being is used up in this expenditure. Being remains constantly available to us. Would we wish to maintain, however, that this use of being, which we constantly rely upon, leaves being so untouched? Is not being at least consumed in use? Does not the indifference of the "is," which occurs in all saying, attest to the wornness of what we thus name?

Being is certainly not grasped, but it is nevertheless worn-out and thus also "empty" and "common." Being is the most worn-out.

"Being" stands everywhere and at each moment in our understanding as what is most self-understood. It is thus the most worn-out coin with which we constantly pay for every relation to beings, without which payment no relation to beings as beings would be allotted us. Being, the most worn-out and the most indifferent! And yet: we do not throw the "is" away; we also never become weary of the being of beings. Even where one might sometimes wish, oneself, no longer to be, ennui pertains only to oneself as this existing human being, but not to being. Even in that most extreme satiety that secretly remains a wishing, and wishes there might *be* the Nothing instead of beings, even there being remains the only thing called upon that resists expenditure and consumption. For also where we expect that it would be preferable for the Nothing *to be*, the last saving grasp is aimed at the most worn-out—at being. Therefore being can never become worn-out to the point of complete exhaustion and disparagement. On the contrary, in the extremity of the desired annihilation of all beings, and precisely here, being must appear. It appears here as something unprecedented and untouched, from out of which stem all beings and even their possible annihilation. Being first lets every being be as such, that means to spring loose and away, to be a being, and as such to be "itself." Being lets every being as such originate. Being is the *origin*.

Being is the emptiest and at the same time a surplus.
Being is the most common of all and at the same time uniqueness.
Being is the most intelligible and at the same time concealment.
Being is the most worn-out and at the same time the origin.

§12. Being is the most reliable and at the same time the non-ground

Whenever, whichever way, and to whatever extent beings become questionable and uncertain to us, we do not doubt being itself. Whether this or that being is, whether this being is so or that being is otherwise, may remain undecided, indeed undecidable in specific cases. Through all of the wavering uncertainty of beings, being, by contrast, offers reliability. For how could we doubt beings in whatever respect if we could not rely in the first place upon what is called "being"?

Being is the most reliable, and so unconditionally reliable that, in all spheres of our comportment toward beings, we do not ever become clear as to the trust we everywhere place upon it.

Nevertheless, if we ever wanted to ground our plans and recourses among beings—our using and shaping of things—immediately upon being, if we wanted to assess the reliability of the everyday according to how being is grounded in its essence there, and how this essence is familiar to us, then we must just as soon experience that none of our intentions and attitudes can be built directly upon being. Being, otherwise constantly used and called upon, offers us no foundation and no ground upon which we can immediately place whatever we erect, undertake, and bring about every day. Being thus appears as the groundless, as something that continually gives way, offers no support, and denies every ground and basis. Being is the refusal of every expectation that it could serve as a ground. Being everywhere turns out to be the *non-ground*.

Being is the most worn-out and at the same time the origin.

Being is the most reliable and at the same time the non-ground.

§13. Being is the most said and at the same time a keeping silent

Because we first depend upon being insofar as we are given over to beings and are released into beings, this dependence constantly and everywhere is put into word. And this not only in the pervasive and immeasurably frequent use of its explicit names, such as "is" and "are" and "was" and "shall be" and "has been." In each "tense-word" of language we name being.

If we say "it rains," we mean that rain "is" here and now. In addition, we name beings in every noun and adjective, and thus name the being of beings along with them. "The war": the being that "is" now. It is sufficient to name a "being," and we mean, in a merely approximate yet portentous thinking, the being of this being. We name being along with it. Being is said along with every word and verbal articulation, if not named each time with its own name. Speaking says being "along with," not as an addition and a supplement that could just as well be left out, but as the pre-giving of what always first permits the naming of beings. Being is "said" even where we silently act, where, among beings, we wordlessly decide about beings, and, without actually naming them, comport ourselves toward beings. In the same way, even where we are left "completely speechless," we "say" being. *Being is the most said in all saying, because everything sayable is only to be said in being* (and only "truth" and its seriousness are sayable).

Must not being, due to its multiple and constant saying, be already so articulated and well-known that its essence lies uncovered before us in complete determinacy? But what if the most said in saying kept its essence secret, if being kept to itself in the disclosure of its essence, and this not only occasionally and incidentally but according to its essence? Then not only would concealment belong to being, but concealment would have a marked relation to "saying" and would be *silence*. Then being would consist in keeping its essence silent. Because being remains the most said in every word, it would be silence *per se*, that essential silence from out of which a word first issues and must issue in breaking this silence. From this break, and as such a break, every word would have its own constellation, and following from this, the stamp of its sound and resonance. *As silence, being would also be the origin of language.*

If this is accurate, then we understand why an animal does not speak and no other "living thing" can speak. The animal does not speak because silence is impossible for it, and an animal cannot be silent because it has no relation to what can be kept silent about, i.e., to keeping silent, i.e., to concealment, i.e., to being. For "speaking," if the word comes from such an origin, is not some arbitrary appearance and condition that we discern in man as one capability among others, like seeing and hearing, grasping and locomotion. For language stands in an essential relation to the uniqueness of being. Being itself obliges us to the next guideword:
Being is the most reliable and at the same time the non-ground.
Being is the most said and at the same time a keeping silent.

§14. *Being is the most forgotten and at the same time remembrance*

It becomes clearer and clearer to us how being everywhere remains the closest in all relations to beings, and yet being is entirely passed over in favor of beings, in whom all willing and knowing seeks its fulfillment. No wonder we forget being on account of beings and their multitude, forget it as something worthy of any consideration at all. Insofar as a claim upon being is awakened and an inquiry about it is made, the indication immediately comes forth that being indeed counts as the most intelligible, but beyond this is not further determinable. Being is thus forgotten in respect to its question-worthiness and indeed so fundamentally forgotten that we even forget this forgetting. It pertains to the essence of forgetting that it forgets itself, i.e., twists itself more and more into its own vortex. Hence, we must admit: *Being is, among all that is worthy of interrogation and consideration, the most forgotten.*

If we wanted to remain exclusively with this observation, being would obviously never and nowhere have to concern us. But if we concede for one moment the possibility, if we once allow the point that being *per se* has sunk into the still concealed Nothing of forgetfulness, if we seriously posit the case that being has been completely stricken from our knowing, how could we then encounter the smallest and most fleeting being as a being, how could we ever experience ourselves as a being?

We constantly comport ourselves toward beings and are beings. We discern not only about ourselves that we are beings, but about our being that we are concerned, one way or another, with ourselves and how we are. Being concerns us, whether it is a matter of the being that we are ourselves or those beings that we are not and never can be. We are always that being that is concerned with being, who, thus concerned and struck, finds in being what is most reliable. Being remains everywhere reliable, and yet, considered in respect to its rank within what is worthy of reflection, it is the most forgotten. Despite this forgottenness, however, it remains in everyday comportment not only the reliable, but is, prior to that, already something that grants us awareness of beings and permits us to be beings in the midst of beings. Being allows us in every respect to be aware of beings and of each in its own way. *Being re-members [Er-innert] us into beings and about beings,* so that everything we encounter, whether experienced as present or past or future, each time first becomes and remains evident as a being through the re-membrance *of* being. Being thus remembers essentially. Being is itself what re-members, *is* the authentic remembrance.

We must indeed consider that being itself is what remembers, not only something *about* which *we* remember, to which we can always return as something already familiar in the sense of Plato's ἀνάμνησις. Plato's doctrine says only how we comport ourselves toward the being of beings, when we assess this comportment according to the relation in which we otherwise stand to "beings." Now, however, we must perceive that being is not an "object" of possible remembrance for us, but is itself what authentically remembers, what allows all awareness of anything that comes into the Open as a being.

Being is the most said and at the same time a keeping silent.
Being is the most forgotten and at the same time remembrance.

§15. *Being is the most constraining and at the same time liberation*

Even though being (as what is emptiest and most worn-out) might sink from the sphere of "reflection" that otherwise remains, and completely disappear into the indifference of forgetting in which even this indifference is annihilated, everywhere being once again constrains us. And indeed it constrains us continually, so that beings meet us and carry us away, surpass us and flatten us, burden us and uplift us. For if, prior to all beings, being and only being allows each to be a being, then each being remains, however it might concern and affect us, infinitely far behind the constraint of being itself. No multitude of beings ever surpasses the "force" that comes from being and presences as being. Even where all beings no longer concern us, become indifferent, and give themselves over to empty caprice, even there the force of being reigns. Because that which constrains surpasses everything in its force, it gives way before no being and in no being, but exacts from each that as a being it remains forced into being. *Being is the most constraining,* wherever, whenever, and however a being might be.

And yet: we do not "detect" the force of being, but at most an impact and a pressing from the side of beings. Despite that constraint, being is as if it "were" rather not "there," and therefore precisely like "the Nothing." We attempt in vain to find being there and yonder. Being plays around us and through us, as if inexperienceable. But this play constantly has in everything the singular univocity of the unique. For is not "being" that which has already placed us "there," where beings as such are differentiated from one another? Is not being that which opens, that which first unlocks the Openness of a "there," in which the possibility is first granted that beings are differentiated from being, that beings *and* being are set apart from each other?

Being first sets being and beings apart, and places us into this apartness and into the free. Placement into this setting apart of being and beings is liberation into belongingness to being. This liberation liberates so that we are free "before" beings and in their midst, free "toward" beings, "free" from them, "free" for them, and thus we have the possibility to be ourselves. Placement into being is *liberation* into freedom. This liberation alone is the essence of freedom.

Being is the most forgotten and at the same time remembrance.
Being is the most constraining and at the same time liberation.

§16. Unifying reflection upon being in the sequence of guidewords

If we pull together the previously attempted reflection upon being in the sequence of the guidewords, we will become attentive and more collected for what at first might only appear like an empty sound:
Being is the emptiest and the most common of all.
Being is the most intelligible and the most worn-out.
Being is the most reliable and the most said.
Being is the most forgotten and the most constraining.
At the same time, however:
Being is a surplus and uniqueness.
Being is concealment and the origin.
Being is the non-ground and a keeping silent.
Being is re-membrance and liberation.
The "is" reveals itself as something that apparently only escapes from *us* as something said, as something that in truth holds *us* in its essence, and yes, even in its non-essence (the forgetting of being).

Are we simply asserting and arranging arbitrary determinations of being here, and using the no less simple device of opposition to multiply each one by its opposite? A decision regarding this plausible opinion must be postponed. Before that, we must get beyond the poverty in which common opinion, and a two-thousand-year-old metaphysical thinking as well, present "being."

We only want to "experience" this: that when we follow the saying μελέτα τὸ πᾶν and consider beings as a whole, we stand immediately in the difference between beings and being, that herewith being announces an essential fullness, assuming that we only begin to think being itself.

But have we now in fact thought being itself?

Recapitulation

Guidewords about Being

1. Being is empty as an abstract concept and at the same time a surplus

In the first attempt to trace this distinction between being and beings, and thereby to illuminate above all what "being" says here, we at first follow the long habituation of a firmly ingrained way of thinking. This expresses itself in the doctrine that being is the name for the "most abstract" of all concepts. Seen thus, the distinction between beings and being, when we attempt to assess it evenly according to both of its "sides," is in truth such that all weight falls on the side of beings. For being is, like a bothersome (if also in a certain respect indispensable) abstraction, only tolerated as an appendage and a shadow of beings. For itself, being is nothing that could evenly and equitably maintain itself "next" to beings and offer a satisfactory basis for reflection. Being is like the fleeting shadow of a cloud floating over the land of beings, without effecting anything or leaving behind any trace. The shadowy character of being confirms, at best, the solidity that belongs solely to beings.

If this is so, then it is also clear wherein, alone, the genuine fulfillment of the guideword μελέτα τὸ πᾶν would consist: namely, in exclusively experiencing and shaping and dealing with beings. The now emerging age of modernity indeed has its undeniable passion in that it grasps all experiencing, pursuing, planning, and constructing of the actual in all respects unconditionally, and that it knows this unconditionedness correctly as the new, and values it as something hitherto not yet willed on earth and as something unique that was never possible until now. The superiority of beings over being has been decided.

Yet the question still remains as to whether or not here, and just here, in this unconditional affirmation of beings (which seems to side exclusively with beings at the expense of being), whether or not here a decision about being holds sway. Thus it remains to be asked whether or not being is precisely something other than merely a name for the most empty concept, whether being is not always and actually a surplus from which all fullness of beings, however they might present themselves, originates. It remains to be asked whether being is not indeed both the emptiness that incontestably shows itself in the most general concept, and the surplus that announces itself to us, for example, in Goethe's verse. Being would then be not only something abstracted and set aside from beings, but contrarily, and at the same time, it would be what exercises its essence in each being everywhere and above all.

2. Being is the most common of all and at the same time uniqueness (The sameness of being and nothing)

In reflecting upon the distinction between beings and being, we asked about being. The previous consideration led to a second guideword about being:

Being is the most common of all and at the same time uniqueness.

We continually encounter in all beings, may they be completely different in content and mode, this uniformity: that they are. Thus it might seem as if being had everywhere dispersed and exhausted itself in being the most commonplace in the land of the most various beings. Because of its uniformity, being was not at all conspicuous to us at first. This "commonness" indeed belongs to being; but being does not exhaust itself in it. For at the same time being is, by contrast, uniqueness. Being presences only as something unique, whereas beings are here this and here that, here the one and not the other. Beings always have their equal. Being, however, is incomparable. Therefore it cannot be said that being is, in the sense of the aforementioned commonality, the same in all beings. Rather, being, as the unique, is always *the Same*. As this sameness, it does not exclude differences. What is in itself and everywhere the same need not, according to its essence, remain merely monotonous. There are various modes of the same being, but there is no various being in the sense that being could break up into something multiple and numerous.

From the development of the Western doctrine of the being of beings (metaphysics) a much-cited proposition has emerged, above all in its scholastic form: *omne ens est unum.* (Every being is one.) To what extent this proposition goes back to Greek thinking about beings, and in what respect it presents a transformation of the same, cannot be discussed here. Only this is to be remembered: that Greek thinking equates beings, τὸ ὄν, early on with τὸ ἕν, the one, and indeed already in pre-Platonic thinking being is distinguished by "unity." Until today, "philosophy" has neglected to reflect at all upon what the ancient thinkers mean with this ἕν. Above all, it does not ask why, at the inception of Western thought, "unity" is so decisively attributed to beings as their essential feature.

The later proposition of scholastic philosophy, *omne ens est unum,* may not be equated with the guideword that has sprung from our reflection: Being is uniqueness. For the former proposition deals with beings (*ens*), not with being as such, and says in truth that beings are always manifold. The proposition means: Every being is always one and as one it is respectively one to another. Therefore each being is always the other to each respective one. *Omne ens est unum,* we can also "translate" by the proposition: Beings are manifold. But the proposition "Being is uniqueness" is spoken from a completely different viewpoint. This seems to be endangered by the Nothing, and certainly insofar as the Nothing is in any way a third *vis-à-vis* beings and being, so that the proposition "Being is the unique over against beings" becomes untenable, but also insofar as the Nothing is in a certain way the other to being.

(In this way Hegel thinks the relation of "being" and "nothing," whereby he remains cognizant that, strictly speaking, he cannot at all address the Nothing as the other to being, because both are taken as the most extreme abstractions of "actuality" and have not yet developed into something (*quale*). Here, Hegel could never risk the proposition: "Actuality" (in his sense) and Nothing are the same. In this respect, however, what is said about the Nothing is meant here, and may not be conflated with Hegel's "identification" of being and nothing.

The citation of the Hegelian "identification" of being and nothing in the essay "What is Metaphysics?" does not mean the adoption of the Hegelian position, but rather intends only to point out that this otherwise alien "identification" was already thought in philosophy.)

Our considerations ought, only in passing, attend to the following: notwithstanding the fact that beings are, the Nothing presences, and "is" in no way the "nullity" that people would gladly cast aside. Ordinary understanding believes, of course, that the Nothing first enters the scene when all beings have been eliminated. However, since in this case even man would be eliminated, no one would remain to think the Nothing, whereupon it is "proven" that the Nothing rests upon fancy and a mere play of understanding—but only so long as one misuses understanding instead of using it only for everyday business. That understanding has its legitimate domain here, no one would want to dispute. Yet, precisely because this is so, it could be doubted whether ordinary understanding, without further ado, has the "legitimacy" to pass judgment upon the essence of the Nothing. Thus it is necessary to remark that the Nothing is indeed the emptiest of the empty, but at the same time it has its equivalent nowhere else. This double characteristic of the Nothing has special meaning for our question. *The Nothing is the emptiest and is unique.*

The same goes for being. Otherwise, the sameness of being and the Nothing would be a strange word, seeming to subsequently strengthen the aforementioned suspicion that being is only a negative and baseless abstraction.

However, to us the Nothing is not a nullity. To recoil in terror of annihilation and to be horrified by devastation is to shrink back from something that cannot be addressed as mere imagination, as something baseless.

On November 2, 1797, Hölderlin wrote to his brother: "The more we are assailed by the Nothing that yawns around us like an abyss or that shapelessly, soullessly and lovelessly haunts us and disperses us from a thousandfold something belonging to society and the activity of men, the more passionate, intense and violent must be the *opposition* from our side. Or must it not?"[7]

But what if the Nothing that horrifies man and displaces him from his usual dallying and evasions were the same as being? Then being would have to announce itself as something horrifying and dreadful, as that which assails us. But we would not gladly accept this. As long as we move within the usual beliefs about being, we leave it aside as something indifferent, and that is already an avoidance of being. This avoidance of being is carried out in many ways, which are not at all recognized as such because the priority of beings claims all thinking, so that even calculating with beings often counts as reflection. Avoidance of being shows itself in the fact that being is taken as the *most intelligible of all that is understandable*. That it comes to this, and can come to this, must, however, rest yet again with being itself. To what extent this is so remains at first unclear. If we have once become aware of our constant flight to reassurance through the "self-understood," then we easily observe everywhere how man at once embeds beings, as yet unexplained, within the sphere of the intelligible. Thus we find it entirely in order when everyone, just as they please, presumes to make judgments about the being of beings according to random notions, immediately current intuitions, and opinions that are barely thought out. On the other hand, one takes it to be entirely natural that, where it is a matter of managing and investigating beings, the trained practitioner, the qualified expert, the appointed leader has the word, and judgment is withheld from the arbitrariness of Everyman.

Reference to the contemporary claims of modern atomic physics to be able to deliver the guiding thread for interpreting the world in general

---

7. F. Hölderlin, *Sämtliche Werke, Historisch-Kritische Ausgabe,* ed. N. v. Hellingrath, F. Seebass, L. v. Pigenot, vol. 2 (1794–1798) (Berlin, second edition, 1923), p. 420.

should make one thing clear: that the fundamental representations of beings that rule in modern physics are elevated to the standard of measure for reflection about the world *per se*, and that in this procedure nothing exceptional and random is seen. People consider it superfluous to consider whether the sketch of beings as a whole has its own system of laws so that it cannot be arbitrarily set to work from anywhere. Modern atomic physics was also named, and only named, in respect to our guiding reflection aimed at the essence of being and the way in which it reveals itself. We are not concerned, here, with expounding a philosophical critique of contemporary physics. For this purpose reflection would have to be aimed differently; it also could not limit itself to an examination of the "law of causality."

When, however, contemporary physics equates an event's having been caused with its predictability, this clearly does not happen incidentally. In respect to this equivalence, one cannot simply affirm that the principle of causality is a principle of beings but predictability is a principle of the knowledge of beings, so that even physics would fall into the error of converting an ontological law into an "epistemological" principle, thus confusing two different realms. The question remains: In what sense is the principle of causality a law of beings? We cannot make do with the naive representation according to which causality would be a law of the actual. Between the naive understanding of causality and the concept of causality in physics stands Kant and his interpretation of causality, which is not incidental, but codetermined by the metaphysical rudiments of modern physics. In our connection, it is not a matter of taking a position in regard to the understanding of causality in modern physics, but of indicating that the hardly noticed attitude which takes the essence of being as self-understood lies at the bottom of the claim of physics, as quantum physics, to be able to found a "quantum biology" and thus, as it were, a "quantum history" and, as it were, a "quantum metaphysics." This reference to the claim of physics, which today also comes correspondingly from biology, should bring into view a sign, among others, indicating that in general "being" means for us the most intelligible.

3. The meaning of the guidewords: Instructions for reflection
upon the difference between being and beings

We are attempting, through a series of guidewords, to raise into know-ing something about the being of beings. And this, for the present, only in order to procure for ourselves, entirely from afar and in a modest way, a preparation for the resolve to follow the ancient saying μελέτα τὸ πᾶν, and in following what is incipient in Western thinking to come nearer and thus to know something of *what*, after all, is said in the inception. In case we are struck by a word from this inceptive saying, we are at least in clearer readiness for the direction toward which we must listen.

It must be observed with respect to misunderstandings already circu-lating that the guidewords about being do not appear as propositions that promulgate a special doctrine or system, or that merely develop a particu-lar "theory" about being. The guidewords are not propositions that can be passed around as assertions "about" a "philosophical standpoint." Taken as such, they would be misunderstood in everything essential.

The guidewords are *instructions for reflection* upon what comes to light when we have a proper eye for what we can do without. And indeed this reflection can be carried out at all times, from all situations, and accord-ing to various forms. It also does not have to cling to the phrasing of what is said here.

The main point is this: to take notice of something neglected, to learn to take notice of it without the hasty urge to immediately seek out utility and purpose. In the realm of this reflection, it is a matter of having the courage not to be as "daring" as the usual and exclusive calculation of what is actual in each case. It is a matter of having the courage to look around the domain of the difference between beings and being and sim-ply to recognize what holds sway here. It is a matter of resisting the nearly ineradicable thought that every such attempt is only a going astray in abstractions, and indeed to resist on grounds of the growing knowledge of being, which might appear to us like the incarnation of all abstraction pure and simple.

At the end we say: *Being is the most said.* For it is said in every word of language, and nevertheless discourse and writing talk for the most part only about beings. This comes to articulation. Even where we actually say the "is" and thus name being, we say the "is" only to assert a being about a being. *Beings are said. Being is kept silent about.* But not by us and on purpose. For we are unable to discover any trace of an intention not to say being. Hence, the keeping silent must indeed come from being itself. Hence, being is a keeping silent about itself, and this is certainly the ground of the possibility of keeping silent and the origin of silence. In this realm of silence, the word first arises each time.

THIRD DIVISION

Being and Man

§17. *The ambivalence of being and the essence of man:*
What casts itself toward us and is cast away

When it was said that being is the most intelligible, most said, most forgotten, wasn't something named that pertains solely to being insofar as it stands subsequently in relation to our understanding, to our saying, to our forgetting? All these things that belong to us, don't they belong to what man, the human subject, is provided with, so that everything that comes into relation with them is immediately given a "subjective" tint? Yet we are supposed to think being itself, therefore being "in itself," therefore we are supposed to think being "objectively."

However, is it true that everything brought into relation to man, and determined from this relation, is thus already "subjective"? And if so, why is the "subjective" immediately burdened with suspicion? The subjective is only where there is a "subject." But the question remains whether man is only a "subject" pure and simple, whether his essence exhausts itself in being a subject. Perhaps only the modern and "most modern" man is a "subject," and perhaps this is due to particular reasons which do not at all guarantee the fact that historical man, in whose history we stand ourselves, was necessarily and always in essence a "subject" and must remain a "subject." In addition to all of this, we would have to discern what it means that man is supposed to be a "subject." How is it that a being could only be objective precisely for *the* man who is a subject? How is it that in the latest modernity an "objectivity" is supposed to be reached that history has never known before? And this only because man has become a subject. Subjectivity surely does not mean the exclusion of truth.

However we might put this question and answer it, the aforenamed determinations of being, according to which it is called the most understood, the most said, the most forgotten, remain nevertheless unequivocally relative to man and human modes of comportment—understanding, saying, forgetting. Being is thought in relation to man and conceived according to a human shape. It is taken "anthropomorphically" and thereby humanized. We do not come into relation with being itself, but at best with what we humans represent to ourselves as being.

But let us leave this difficulty aside and allow the danger to persist that instead of thinking being itself we everywhere only "humanize" being. This humanization of being could still grant us a glimpse into being itself, although a murky one. However, a far greater reservation arises before us that threatens to annihilate the entire reflection upon being we are now attempting.

We say being "*is*" the emptiest, "*is*" a keeping silent, "*is*" the most intelligible, "*is*" a surplus. Being "*is*"—indeed, does being not become irrevocably a being in this saying, when we address it as something that "is"? Does it not become what it is supposed to be differentiated from? We may multiply assertions about being into infinity, but they become untenable at the first step because an assertion in the form of "being is . . . " already destroys what we want to apprehend: *being as distinct from beings.* But if being immediately appears to us as what this and that "is," can it ever at all become manifest *as being,* regardless of whether we, in representing being, lend it human characteristics or not? Everywhere and every time, wherever and whenever being is named, only beings are immediately meant.

From here, it looks as though the "natural" way of thinking attains its full justification. Ordinary opinion sticks to beings and declares that being, so-called, is an "abstraction," a way of speaking that corresponds to nothing and makes fools of all thinkers who chase after it. It subsequently becomes clear how far the neglect of being and the forgetting of its question-worthiness perhaps follow from a genuine insight: that in respect to being in general nothing serious can be asked. Thus it remains true: only beings "are."

To be sure—only beings, but what "is" with them? They, beings, "are." But what does it mean, they "are"? What does being consist of? What is the proposition "beings *are*" supposed to mean if we heed the above mentioned misgivings, cast being aside as an abstraction, even obliterate it, and then only allow beings to count? Then only "beings" remain. But what does it mean that beings "remain"—does it mean anything other than that beings and only "beings" "are"? And if we want only to hold fast to beings, to avoid the "abstraction" of being, to remain steadfast and exclusively with beings, and accordingly say beings are beings, then we also still say the "is" and thus still think in terms of being. Being continually overtakes us as that which we can never not think.

So we stand between two equally unavoidable limits. On the one side, we immediately make being into a being when we think it and say of it "being 'is,'" thus disavowing the proper work of being: *we cast being away from us.* On the other side, however, we can never disavow "being" and the "is" wherever we experience a being. For how should a being be in each case a being for us without our experiencing it *as* a *being*, without our experiencing it in respect to its being?

Being has already cast itself over us and toward us. Being: casting itself toward us and cast away by us. This looks like a "contradiction." However, we do not wish to capture what opens up here in a formal schema of formal thinking. Everything would merely become weakened in its essence, and essence-less, under the appearance of a "paradoxical" formula. On the other hand, we must attempt to experience that, located between both limits, we are placed into a peculiar abode from which there is no way out. But in finding ourselves placed into this impasse, we also become aware that such an extreme impasse could perhaps stem from being itself. Indeed, without exception the guidewords indicate a peculiar ambivalence of being.

If, in the manner just presented, thinking encounters insurmountable difficulties, and sees itself placed into a situation where there is no way out, then it can yet deliver itself from peril in the way previous thinking has done. We have already refrained from the nearest available technique of discerning a contradiction and playing, so to speak, with a "paradox." For relinquishing thought is the most deplorable way for thought to accomplish its task. Nevertheless, according to the way of thinking practiced until now in the otherwise usual questions of philosophy, one could undertake still other and subsequent reflections in respect to the impasse now arrived at. In view of this situation where there is no way out, where, on the one hand, being cannot be avoided, and, on the other hand, investigating being immediately makes it into a "being" and thus destroys its essence, one gives up the question of being altogether and declares it to be a pseudoquestion. Or else one decides to acknowledge the now exposed impasse ("aporia"). One must then come to terms with it in some way. In such cases, the popular technique of making a virtue of necessity offers itself as a salvation. Accordingly, we could say in respect to our impasse that being itself forces us into this situation with no way out and even brings it about. Therefore, being would show itself to be what is represented as at once both unavoidable and yet ungraspable. What it shows itself to be in this way, this impasse, is precisely its essence. The impasse that being brings with it is being's own mark of distinction. Therefore, let us take the impasse as the predicate with whose help the decisive assertion about being can be won. It states: Being is every time, with every attempt to think it, converted into a being and thus destroyed in its essence; and yet being, as distinguished from all beings, cannot be denied. Being itself has just this kind of essence: it brings human thinking into an impasse. When we know that, we already know something essential about being.

Do we truly know "something" essential about being, or do we merely discern what happens to us and our thinking when we try to comprehend being? Indeed, the only thing we attain is an insight into our incapacity to comprehend being. As long as we let it rest with an account of the aforementioned impasse, we ascertain an "aporia." With this determination, which looks like an important insight, we close our eyes to the abode in which, despite all looking away, we remain. For we lay a claim to being in all our comportments toward beings. But we can consider still another possible attitude, where we neither close our eyes to the impasse nor pass it and its discernment off as the ultimate culmination of wisdom, where we first actually look around in this situation where there is no way out and banish all haste to escape from it.

In saying something about being we make it into a "being" and thus cast it away. But being has always already cast itself toward us. *Casting-away and at the same time casting-toward,* no way out in any direction. What if the absence of every way out were a sign that we may no longer think of ways out, and that means we first establish a footing and become at home in this supposedly impassable place, instead of chasing after the usual "escape routes"? What if the "escape routes" we lay claim to stem from claims that remain inappropriate to the essence of being, and originate from our passion for beings? What if the impasse into which being places us when we want to comprehend it must first be perceived as a sign that points toward where we are already placed in principle, since we comport ourselves toward beings?

This place means a still concealed abode, to which the essence of our history owes its origin. We do not enter this abode as long as we try to make it discernable through a historiological depiction of historiologically recognizable happenings. For this abode is the one that concerns our essence. Whether we recognize and know it, or have only contemplated it, remains entirely undecided.

What if we did not know where we are and who we are? What if all previous answers to the questions of who we are were merely based upon the repeated application of an answer given long ago, an answer that does not at all correspond to what is perhaps asked in the question, now touched upon, of who we are? For we do not now ask about ourselves "as human," assuming we understand this name in its traditional meaning. According to this meaning, man is a kind of "organism" (animal, ζῷον) that exists among others on the inhabited earth and in the universe. We know this organism, especially since we ourselves are of this type. There is a whole contingent of "sciences" that give information about this organism—named man—and we collect them together under the name "anthropology." There are books with presumptuous titles, e.g., "Man," that claim to know who man is—as if the opinion of the American pseudophilosophy (which contemporary German science all too keenly adopts) already presented the truth about man.

We are free to locate this organism "man" in the most varied, narrower or broader domains, e.g., within the narrower or broader spheres of his everyday activities, or within the widest domain of the earth, where it is regarded as one orb among millions of others in the universe. Nietzsche says in the beginning of the essay "On Truth and Lies in a Nonmoral Sense":

> Once upon a time, in some out of the way corner of that universe which is dispersed into numberless twinkling solar systems, there was a star upon which clever beasts invented knowing. That was the most arrogant and mendacious minute of "world history," but nevertheless, it was only a minute. After nature had drawn a few breaths, the star cooled and congealed, and the clever beasts had to die.[8]

Man: an animal appearing "in nature," fitted out with cleverness (reason): *animal rationale*.

§18. The historicality of being and the historically essential abode of man

We are not asking here about man as a natural entity, nor about man as a "rational entity," which is the same. We are not at all asking about man as a being found among other beings. We are also not asking about man insofar as he stands in relation to beings. We are asking about that entity named "man" in such a way that we bring only this into experience as his sole determination: that he stands in an abode laid out by being itself. That means in such an abode that until now—with the assistance of usual ways of thinking—we could only call an "impasse." We now experience humanity in an abode where being reveals its inescapability as what is cast toward us, and therein reveals its inviolability. We experience an abode where being gives itself up, in its own self-

---

8. F. Nietzsche, *Nachgelassene Werke, Aus den Jahren 1872/73–1875/76; Nietzsches werke*, part 2, vol. X, 3: "Wahrheit und Lüge im aussermoralischen Sinne" (Leipzig, 1903), p. 189. English translation: "On Truth and Lies in a Nonmoral Sense," *Philosophy and Truth: Selections from Nietzsche's Notebooks of the Early 1870s*, trans. and ed. Daniel Breazeale (Atlantic Highlands: Humanities Press, 1979), p. 79.

destruction, so to speak, when being immediately becomes a being through all representing and thinking of it.

We experience this, that means we rid ourselves of the apparent possibilities for avoiding this abode. We begin by renouncing the attempt to find support through any kind of appeal to this or that being in order to "have done" with being, or to put forward an excuse so that we would not have to ask about being in the first place. Nonetheless, we do not deny that the experience of this abode contains an exacting expectation that cannot be assessed according to the usual demands placed upon "reflection." The exacting expectation of such an experience does not stem from us, as if it were merely the result of our deliberations, concocted from some philosophical "standpoint." This demand to experience the abode of historical man, alluded to above, originates from a claim of being itself, where the perdurance of man (himself) lies anchored. The claim comes from the still concealed essence of history. Hence this demand to experience the essential abode of historical man is strange. We should in no respect minimize this strangeness. We want to hold it fast, and that means, first of all: we want to concede that we never experience the slightest thing about the essential abode of historical man arbitrarily and unprepared, never unbidden and never through the aid of a mere curiosity that suddenly arises in us. We admit that for such an experience of history we need history itself to make us remember and to give us hints for reflection. Such a reflection grants us remembrance of the first inception of Western thought.

Why that is so, only this inception itself can tell us, provided we allow ourselves to be told something essential.

§19. Remembrance into the first inception of Western thinking is reflection upon being, is grasping the ground

For many reasons, certainly, we are immediately overtaken by a series of partially familiar considerations, two of which should be mentioned but not discussed in detail. People will say: The first inception of Western thinking is unattainable for us, and if it were historiologically attainable it would remain inoperative. What is making present something long past supposed to accomplish for us?

Indeed, if this making present pertained only to a being that previously was and is now no longer, if this making present pertained to a sequence of thought-acts carried out by thinkers who lived in the past, then we would be fixing our search upon something that has disappeared. However, we do not want to make a past being live again in the present. On the contrary, we want to become aware of being. In reflection, we remember being and the way it inceptively presences, and presences still as the inception, without thereby ever becoming a present being. The inception is certainly something that has been but not something past. What is past is always a no-longer-being, but what has been is being that still presences but is concealed in its incipience.

The concealedness of the inception does not mean the inception has been covered over. It implies only the peculiarity of an inception that first strikes us from its nearness, that cannot be experienced in the realm of what is self-evident. Perhaps this inception of being is closer to us than everything we know and allow as the nearest; closer, that is, than all beings, which, as actual, seem to absorb into themselves and rule over everything.

The past is past. That means the former beings are no longer beings. All historiology deals with beings that are no longer. No historiological presentation is ever capable of making a former being into the being it was. Everything past is only something that has passed away. But the passing away of beings occurs in the essential realm of being. This does not, of course, "subsist" somewhere "in itself," but is what is properly historical in the past, the imperishable, and that means it is an incipiently having been and an incipiently presencing again.

Remembrance of the inception is not concerned with beings and what is past, but with what has been, and that means with what still presences, being. Perhaps the inception continues to appear, for the most part, so completely as something unattainable because it is overly close, so that we have continually overlooked it due to its nearness. Perhaps it belongs to the peculiarity of the abode in which our historical essence remains bound that, though we certainly do not lack sight and sense for the closest

of all proximities, sight and sense are nevertheless suppressed, and suppressed by the power of the actual which has presumed to become not
only the measure for each respective being, but for being.

To be sure, we would be deluded if we wanted to deny that every
attempt to bring the remembrance of the first inception of Western thinking to a decision, directly and without preparation, belongs to the realm
of fantasy. We will therefore forgo any extensive justifications of such an
attempt. Besides, these justifications in advance of any attempt always
remain meaningless if the attempt at such a remembrance is not actually
first carried out. We must go even further and immediately admit that
such a remembering return into the first inception of Western thinking
brings with it all the signs of violence.

To think back into the inception as what has been and still presences,
into what alone, therefore, has a yet-to-come (because a casting-toward
belongs to its essence)—to remember into the inception—means to
gather all reflection toward the "ground," to grasp the "ground." What
ground means here, we find out most easily from the usage that speaks of
a fore-ground, a back-ground and a middle ground (to touch only upon
the "spatial"). Here, ground is the inclusion that gathers out of itself and
into itself, a gathering that grants the Open where all beings are.
"Ground" means being itself and this is the inception.

Recapitulation

1. The discordant essence in the relation of man to being:
The casting-toward and casting-away of being

The guidewords say of being every time: Being "is" . . . a surplus,
"is" concealment, "is" liberation. Being "is" . . . this and that. That
about which we say, "it is," is thereby addressed as a being. To say of
being that it, being, is . . . unintentionally converts being into a being.
Saying thus speaks as if it knew nothing of being. Being is cast away in
saying, by saying, through the word about being, through every word
about being. This casting away of being, however, can never relinquish

being. For being has cast itself toward us as the "light" in which a being always appears as a being. Furthermore, we are incapable of encountering this casting-toward in such a way that it could ever become irrelevant, since we never, in our comportment toward beings, experience their being as if it were a being among the rest.

The casting-toward of being and the casting-away of being are equally essential. Neither can push the other into essencelessness. We ourselves can initiate nothing against being's casting-toward, nor do we want to. At the same time, however, being withdraws from us when we attempt to actually say it. We then refer only to beings. Being has singularly burst open our own human essence. We belong to being, and yet not. We reside in the realm of being and yet are not directly allowed in. We are, as it were, homeless in our ownmost homeland, assuming we may thus name our own essence. We reside in a realm that is constantly permeated by the casting-toward and the casting-away of being. To be sure, we hardly ever pay attention to this characteristic of our abode, but we now ask: "where" are we "there," when we are thus placed into such an abode? (—the answer in terms of the history of being [seyn] says: in being—there—[Da-sein]).

Is this abode only a strange addition to our otherwise univocally determined and ultimately secured human essence, an essence whose situation can indeed be historiologically summed up and depicted? Or is this abode in being that where*in* and where*from* the essential mode, essential rank, and essential primordiality of our historical human essence can, always for the first time and every time differently, decide themselves? If it were so, we would remain away from the essential decision about ourselves as long as we disavow this abode in being, and in its place register only situations of humanity that are "intellectual" and taken from the "history of ideas." Then the question would be whether man has ever been decisively given over into the realm of decision belonging to his own essence, so that he shares in the grounding of his historical essence and does not merely busy himself with his "historical missions." Then it would be completely doubtful whether we can already know who we are, whether we can know this at all with the present claims of thinking. Then the long familiar acquaintance with man, common to everyone, would be no guarantee that man holds himself in the right position to *ask,* in an adequate, essentially legitimate way, who he is—not even to mention the ability to find an answer that would possess the sustaining power to bring the essence of man to its fulfillment in a historical humanity.

But are we not putting artificial and contrived obstacles in the way, because now, in the reflection upon being, we have found the relation of being to man so ambivalent? But let us leave aside this discordant essence in the relation of man to being. After all, what can disturb us about the fact that being casts itself toward us and we immediately cast it away, even though we lay claim to it? Let us completely leave aside the relation of man to being, let us consider what ordinarily and hastily suffices for the moment.

If we consider the place of man within beings, then at once a reassuring situation shows itself: the essence of man has been decided long ago. Namely, man is an "organism" and indeed an "organism" that can invent, build, and make use of machines, an organism that can *reckon* with things, an organism that can put *everything whatsoever* into its calculation and computation, into the ratio. Man is the organism with the gift of reason. Therefore, man can demand that everything in the world happen "logically."

In this demand that there be a world of "reason," a danger for this organism "man" might reveal itself, i.e., that the organism deifies "reason," as first happened already in the course of modernity, in the first French Revolution. But the organism "man" can only confront this danger when it does not become apparent in the mere calculation of life, but gives "life" itself an open course for its stream. "Life" is not, for man, an object standing opposite him. "Life" is also not, for man, a process running its course behind him. Rather, life is what *life itself* accomplishes, enjoys, survives and what, like a river, it guides through itself and carries by its own stream. Life is, as they have said and taught since the nineteenth century, *"lived experience"* [*"Erlebnis"*]. And life is not only occasionally a "lived experience," but is a continuous chain of "lived experiences." A humanity guided by reason will adjust its computation to the fact that this chain of lived experiences never ends. (Thus it can get to the point where life veritably "overflows" with "lived experiences." We do not by any means have to limit ourselves to mere "lived experiences." One can capture them in reports. One already learns this at school.)

Of course, here the opposite danger arises for the "rational organism" named man, not that reason now tumbles over itself, but that everything "is" still only what is "lived" ["*erlebt*"]. But if the right balance between the "calculability" of life and the drunkenness of lived experience belonging to life's urge is found, indeed even if this balance cannot immediately be found in all places and at all times, it is nevertheless clearly shown that the essence of man is securely delimited: man is the presencing animal (—*animal rationale*—).

Besides, today a large contingent of sciences stands at the disposal of the secured human essence, all of which provide information about man. Today we have anthropology. How should we not know who man is? For a long time now we have had the diploma in mechanical engineering, electronics, sewage and waste disposal, and similar things. We have a diploma in political economy, and lately the diploma in forestry, and now we are getting the diploma in psychology. Soon we will be able to read off of tables and graphs what the Americans have clearly sought for decades by means of the psychology diploma: the determination of what man is and how he can be most efficiently and effectively used, in the most appropriate place, without loss of time or energy. But perhaps the question of who man is has already been decided before all psychology diplomas. Anthropology and psychology diplomas only make organized use of what has been decided. The decision is the one that has been long familiar: *Homo est animal rationale.* Man is the rational animal. (For this reason, because computation and reason are involved, man is also capable of what an animal can never achieve, that is, he can sink below the animal.)

If humanity has thus been established in its essence, what is a reflection upon the relation of man to being supposed to accomplish? Does not such reflection upon being run counter to every natural self-consciousness of man? Moreover, the determination of man (*animal rationale*) does not exclude the possibility that the consideration of man will be expanded. One can examine man in his various spheres of life, thus in his relations to beings.

2. Remembrance into the first inception is placement into still presencing being, is grasping it as the ground

Reflection upon being is remembrance into the first inception of Western thinking. Remembrance into the first inception is a fore-thinking into the more incipient inception. Remembrance is no historiological activity with the past, as if it wanted to make present, from outside and from what is later, what earlier thinkers "believed" "about" being. Remembrance is placement into being itself, which still presences, even though all previous beings are past. Indeed, even talk about placement into being is misleading because it suggests we are not yet placed into being, while being yet remains closer to us than everything nearest and farther than all that is farthest. We only appear to escape being in favor and for the sake of beings, whose density fills every openness. Hence it is not first a matter of being placed into being, it is a matter of becoming aware of our essential abode in being, and becoming genuinely aware of being beforehand.

Becoming aware of being means something other than attempting to raise being into consciousness. Moreover, this becoming-aware is not a lost representation of what one vaguely does or does not imagine under the "concept" of "being." *To grasp being means grasping the ground.* Here, grasping [*Begreifen*] means "being included" ["*inbegriffen werden*"] in being by being. Grasping means a transformation of humanity from out of its essential relation to being, before that the readiness for such a change, before that the preparation for this readiness, before that attending to this preparation, before that the impulse to such a preparation, before that the first remembrance into being. Everything that can be attempted to this end remains "preliminary." But perhaps the preliminary [*das Vor-läufige*] is also an extending-in-advance [*ein Voraus-laufen*] into a future of history. Only the initiating and incipient pertains to the future; what is present is always already past. The inception knows no haste. Whither should it hasten, since everything incipient is only incipient if it can rest in itself? Reflection into the inception is thus also an unhurried thinking that never comes too late and at best comes too early.

PART TWO

The Incipient Saying of Being in
the Fragment of Anaximander

*§20. The conflicting intentions of philological tradition and
philosophical translation*

From the first inception of Western thinking a saying is handed down
to us that we for once just once want to hear. The saying belongs to the
Greek thinker Anaximander, who lived from approximately 610 to 540.
The saying states:

ἐξ ὧν δὲ ἡ γένεσίς ἐστι τοῖς οὖσι, καὶ τὴν φθορὰν εἰς ταῦτα
γίνεσθαι κατὰ τὸ χρεών· διδόναι γὰρ αὐτὰ δίκην καὶ τίσιν ἀλλή-
λοις τῆς ἀδικίας κατὰ τὴν τοῦ χρόνου τάξιν.

The translation, which as such is unavoidably already an interpretation,
we will render into a formulation including some elucidating words that
go beyond an exactly "literal" reproduction. We translate:

Whence emergence is for what respectively presences also an eluding into
this (as into the Same), emerges accordingly the compelling need; there is
namely what presences itself (from itself), the fit, and each is respected
(acknowledged) by the other, (all of this) from overcoming the unfit according to the allotment of temporalizing by time.

That this saying came to be handed down to us is more important than
the question as to how this handing down succeeded and can be verified
and supported in detail. For this saying owes its being handed down to
the gravity of its own truth.

We will concern ourselves first with the truth of this saying, which
means the truth of what it puts into words. We will first consider the
essence of what is generally spoken about here. In this approach, we
consciously disregard the requirements of historical-philological scholarship and admit that we are left exposed to the charge of being unschol-

arly. For "scholarship" will demand a procedure that directly conflicts with the one followed here, a procedure that can best be characterized by an assertion from philology, which provides the following explanation:

> The precise reproduction and clear understanding of the original text of this source material, handed down in multiple fragments, is the presupposition and point of departure for any investigation that has tracing the fundamental lines of the Anaximandrian philosophy as its goal.[9]

In regard to this apparently illuminating and totally flawless explanation, only the following is to be noted. In the first place, we do not claim to be tracing "the fundamental lines of the Anaximandrian philosophy." It is possible, perhaps, to establish the "fundamental lines of a philosophy" in regard to a philosophy professor of the nineteenth and twentieth centuries, but this presents the sheerest nonsense in respect to a thinker of the inception. Second, we entrust the "clear understanding of the original text" to a calm reflection, upon whose path this understanding should be won in a different way than as a "point of departure" for tracing a "philosophy." It should be won through a clear understanding of what the words say.

With these two remarks we indeed claim to be "more philological" than this thoughtless type of "scientific philology." Here, "more philological" means more aware in respect to the essential inner conditions of every historiological interpretation, aware that they are nothing without a decisive fundamental relation to history, and that without this relation all philological exactness remains a mere game.

Perhaps the translation can already put a glimmer of the inexhaustible strangeness of this saying into words. The translation does not at all intend to bring the saying "closer" to us, if bringing "closer" means smuggling this saying into the zone of common intelligibility. On the contrary, the translation should move the saying away from us into what is strange and estranging, and allow it to remain there. For, in addition, the interpretation attempted afterwards is not concerned with making the

---

9. K. Deichgräber, "Anaximander von Milet," *Hermes* 75 (1940), 10–19.

saying accessible to us, to cut it down to our own measure. We should experience ourselves as excluded from the saying, as distanced and definitively distanced from what the saying says and, as such a saying, *is*.

But "distanced" does not mean without all relation. On the contrary, there is a distance that brings us nearer than the disrespectful intrusiveness that characterizes all historiology [*Historie*], not to mention the so-called topical approach to historiological writing.

First of all, it is a matter of fending off a tactless familiarity with the incipient and awakening to the insight that precisely the later erudition and ensuing "progress" diminish the incipient more and more, feel themselves at home with the insignificant, and thus remain insignificant themselves compared to the secret frightfulness adhering to the shape of everything incipient.

Ages that see in history only what is past and continually degrade this past as something that just naturally prepares inadequate pre-formations of what is attained in the present are not yet, and that means never, ripe for the essence of history [*Geschichte*]. They remain victim to historiology and thus continually busy themselves with the transformation of 'historical depictions' and take these activities for 'political' 'deeds.' That these deeds are accomplished on the basis of preceding but also vigorously disparaged investigations increases all the more their heroic nature.

§21. Nietzsche's and Diels's renderings of the fragment as the standard for interpretations current today

To make clearer, that is, firmer, what is estranging about the translation (which also remains an attempt), two other renderings may be cited. They should allow for a comparison, and thus to those without a mastery of the Greek language, and, above all, of the way of inceptive thinking, they should also allow a small occasion for one's own reflection. With this in view, not just any renderings will be given, but two that are respectively different in testimonial power even though they are in essential agreement, a fact that likewise has a special significance.

The first of the renderings to be cited stems from Nietzsche, from his manuscript of a treatise entitled *Philosophy in the Tragic Age of the Greeks*, completed in the spring of 1873. In the winter semester of 1869/70, Nietzsche had already held a 'lecture course' in Basel on "The Pre-Platonic Philosophers with an Interpretation of Selected Fragments." Nietzsche himself never published the manuscript, which was finished in 1873. It was first published thirty years later and three years after his death. Nietzsche's rendering runs:

> Where the source of things is, to that place they must also pass away, according to necessity, for they must pay penance and be judged for their injustices, in accordance with the ordinance of time.[10]

In 1903, the same year Nietzsche's treatise first became known, the first collection of *Fragments of the Presocratics* by Herman Diels appeared, prepared according to the methods of modern classical philology. (The since expanded edition contains the standard texts of the fragments of pre-Platonic thinking.)

Diels renders the fragment of Anaximander as follows:

> . . . the source from which existing things derive their existence is also that to which they return at their destruction, according to necessity, for they give justice and make reparation to one another for their injustice, according to the arrangement of Time.[11]

Both of these renderings have remained a standard for interpretations current today. Their specific character should be mentioned briefly, because it is best recognized thereby how far the supposedly scientific interpretation has already forgotten every critique before taking its first step, and made thoughtlessness into its principle.

According to its 'first part' the fragment talks about the coming to be

---

10. F. Nietzsche, *Nachgelassene Werke, Aus den Jahren 1872/73–1875/76; Nietzsches Werke,* part 2, vol. X, 3 (Leipzig, 1903), p. 26. English translation: *Philosophy in the Tragic Age of the Greeks,* trans. Marianne Cowan (South Bend: Gateway, 1962), p. 45.
11. H. Diels, *Die Fragmente der Vorsokratiker,* 1st ed. Berlin, 1903), p. 81. English translation: *Ancilla to the Pre-Socratic Philosophers: A Complete Translation of the Fragments in Diels' 'Fragmente der Vorsokratiker,'* trans. Kathleen Freeman (Cambridge: Harvard University Press, 1966), p. 19.

and the passing away of things, and that means the world, and that means the cosmos. Such a consideration is, according to today's usual way of thinking, purely 'physical' in the widest sense. (We also saw on another occasion how today's physics strives to establish freedom as a 'natural-scientific', i.e. physical, fact.)

The second part of the Anaximander fragment talks about "punishment" and "recompense" and "recklessness" and "injustice," thus about 'juridical' and 'ethical', 'moral' and 'immoral' things, according to the contemporary notions. Hence one thing is clear for today's common sense: in this fragment a "physical law of the universe" is expressed "in ethical and juridical notions." And since the entire passage obviously intends to explain reality from an ultimate cause, and since one can also grasp such notions as 'religious' and can call its corresponding assertion 'theological', this passage does not lack a religious and theological moment. Thus we read at the end of an essay on Anaximander from the year 1940 the following: "From the unity of a great religious, ethical, rational and physical thought arises the first great philosophical construct of mind, the achievement of the Milesian Anaximander."

We do not want to spend our time refuting this "great" piece of nonsense. However, it becomes obvious and unworthy of a special refutation when we consider two things. First, at that time there was no physics and therefore no physical thinking, no ethics and therefore no ethical thinking, no rationalism and therefore no rational thinking, no jurisprudence and therefore no juridical thinking. Indeed, the passage does not even contain a "philosophy" and therefore no "philosophical construct of mind." Secondly, however, the fragment speaks from the original homogeneity of the uniqueness belonging to an incipient thinking. This unity neither contains the later differentiations within itself, nor is it the undeveloped pre-formation of the same, but is unique unto itself.

We do not intend to hold the author of the essay accountable for the results of research, but we should indicate how thoughtlessly one interprets from notions of physics, ethics, jurisprudence, and theology without ever asking whether the orientation upon such notions makes any sense here, not to mention whether or not it is justified. When, by contrast, we attempt to elucidate the thoughts of a thinker by thinking through his problematic, and when, in this attempt, concepts become necessary that are inaccessible to the normal brain of a philologist, then the horror over philosophical constructions and whimsicalities is great. In order to avoid the crudest misunderstandings we note that philosophy should not think any better of itself than philology. Nor should it be said that philology is 'worthless'. Rather, one thing should be brought to notice by this observation:

A passage such as the word of Anaximander demands first of all that we disregard what is familiar to us from our knowledge and world-interpretations. But by not bringing in physical, ethical, juridical, theological, *and* "philosophical notions" we have only accomplished something negative. Something else is required above all: a simple listening for that about which something is said. Perhaps it is the greatest and in many respects the most ineradicable fate of all interpreters, and especially those who practice interpretation as a "business," that from the outset they do not allow themselves to say anything about what they interpret, but conduct themselves as the cleverer ones. This danger, moreover, is especially great in respect to the inceptions of Western thinking. For how easily a broadly educated man of the nineteenth and twentieth centuries comes to think that, precisely in relation to his advanced knowledge, those inceptions of thought must have been elementary, or, as one also says, 'primitive.' The fact that at the same time they also speak of the 'considerable' 'achievements' presented by this incipient thinking does nothing to mitigate the peculiar presumptuousness of those who come later. In bestowing such praise upon the ancient thinkers, the total arrogance of the latecomers expresses itself completely. However, for most it is difficult, nay impossible, to free themselves from the hazy sphere of this explicit (and above all implicit) presumption. We succeed in this only occasionally, when we take the trouble beforehand to carry out some trace of a reflection about what is said in the word to be interpreted. Because everything depends upon this reflection, the previous consideration of being and the distinction between beings and being is always more essential than knowledge of the results of philological research.

However, that reflection must not mislead us into imagining we are now in possession of a key that would open the gates to the truth of this passage, if only we turned it properly in the lock.

Recapitulation

The remembering return into the inception of Western thinking— listening to the fragment of Anaximander

Remembrance into the inception listens first to the fragment of Anaximander. The translation attempted here contains an interpretation of the saying that has originated purely from reflection upon being. This translation can be appropriated and its "truth" verified only in confrontation with this reflection, and that means by reflecting along with it.

For contrast, we cite the translation by Nietzsche and that from the *Fragments of the Presocratics*, first published by Hermann Diels. Anaximander says:

ἐξ ὧν δὲ ἡ γένεσίς ἐστι τοῖς οὖσι, καὶ τὴν φθορὰν εἰς ταῦτα γίνεσθαι κατὰ τὸ χρεών· διδόναι γὰρ αὐτὰ δίκην καὶ τίσιν ἀλλή-λοις τῆς ἀδικίας κατὰ τὴν τοῦ χρόνου τάξιν.

We translate:

Whence emergence is for what respectively presences also an eluding into this (as into the Same), emerges accordingly the compelling need; there is namely what presences itself (from itself), the fit, and each is respected (acknowledged) by the other, (all of this) from overcoming the unfit according to the allotment of temporalizing by time.

Being is overly near. All talk about it as near and as closest has already distanced it, for the nearest proximity already essentially includes distance. Being never stands back from us, because it is that into which we are placed.

Because being is in this way overly near, ever-hasty man is seldom capable of taking what permeates his essence, truthfully and simply, into his knowing: being, the incipient enjoinment [*Verfügung*]. All beings and all relations to beings are given over to being. In the first inception of thought, being is brought into knowing as τὸ χρεών—the compelling need, and that means it is anticipated as this necessity before all knowing. To this essence of being, holding sway as the compelling need, corresponds the demand of the motto μελέτα τὸ πᾶν: "Take into care beings as a whole." Only the pure necessity, which is at the same time liberation into freedom, can lay claim to what is meant by "care." "Take into care . . . " We say now and in the future: Be constant in being! Stand in being!

§22. Reflection upon the incipient saying of being in the fragment of Anaximander

a) Suppositions regarding the relation between the two sentences

What does the fragment of Anaximander say? To be able to listen in the right direction from the outset, we must note that the fragment consists of two sentences. The division is indicated by διδόναι γὰρ αὐτά ("there is namely what presences itself . . . "). But we cannot immediately decide how we are to think the relation between the two sentences. Only one thing remains clear, that the second does not just repeat what is said by the first.

The sentences do not say the same thing, but nevertheless they supposedly say something about the same thing. That there is a difference between the two sentences is shown by the beginning of the second. It is introduced with a γάρ ("for," "namely"). Thus one would like to suppose that the second sentence gives the subsequent ground for the first. But perhaps everything is vice versa. Perhaps the first sentence gives the "ground" for the second, which then expresses a consequence of what is named in the first. Then perhaps we must let all possible caution prevail when we talk directly about "grounds." For what "ground" could possibly mean here must determine itself from the essence of the ground, about which everything is said in the fragment. Perhaps we must completely forgo all modes of thinking familiar to us. At the risk of getting stuck on the surface at first, we must attempt to actually think through both sentences in their content.

b) The saying about being occurs in correspondences: The *first*
sentence thinks being as τὸ χρεών in correspondence with
the inception as threefold enjoinment

The first sentence talks about γένεσις and φθορά; usually we translate these words with "coming to be" and "passing away" (going under,
for Nietzsche). "Coming to be" and "passing away" are names for the
alternating course of all things. We think, however, that "coming to be
and passing away" (wherein precisely the "movement" of things stands
out) are in themselves intelligible "processes," for they are the most familiar "occurrences." Who is not familiar with "coming to be and passing away"? And who does not know that "coming to be and passing
away" take place everywhere and at all times? In what way particular
things come to be and by what causes they each go under may remain
mysterious and in various respects uninvestigated. But the process of
coming to be and passing away is itself indeed a matter of fact that we, as
they say today, "experience" [*erleben*], and, to be sure, in the most diverse
spheres of the actual.

And yet, what does this mean: "coming to be" and "passing away"?
Above all, what do γένεσις and φθορά mean? How are we ever to think
in Greek what one immediately calls "coming to be and passing away"?

Our translation should point the way. Γένεσις: emergence; φθορά:
elusion. The last-mentioned word says more clearly that it is a question of
evasion, meaning going away, as distinguished from coming forth.
"Away" and "forth" demand a more precise stipulation of "whence"
"away" and "whither" "forth" evasion and emergence and what they
are. If we think in the Greek way, thus incipiently, we must necessarily
think this "whither forth" and "whence away" along with emergence
and elusion.

Now, the fragment not only speaks indeterminately about γένεσις and
φθορά, but both are grasped as something that is peculiar to ἔστιν τοῖς
οὖσι, to what respectively presences. Τὰ ὄντα, that means not only
"things" but each and every being. Yet, we do not translate τοῖς οὖσι
with "to beings," but with "to what respectively presences." We want to
name that through which what we call "beings" distinguish themselves

for all Greek (and especially incipient) thinking. Beings are—thought in Greek—what presences. What emerges and evades emerges into presence and goes away out of presence.

(We know in the meantime that we constantly name beings and in many ways, but when we are asked conversely what the "being" of beings is supposed to mean, we are without a clue. Or people bring forward the most manifold "explanations," which only attest once again to how completely being and its essence flits away from us into the essenceless. Will fact-crazed modernity ever properly grasp or want to grasp the fact that being flits away? Indeed, can it want to grasp it at all? The Greeks, at the inception, think differently because they think more simply and decisively.)

The Greek word for beings is used in the plural where something double is named: beings as a whole and the single being that in each case belongs to this whole. But nothing is said about beings except that "emergence" is peculiar to them and that elusion emerges from them. Thus we are talking about what is peculiar to beings, and that is the *being* of beings.

However, emergence and evasion are names for alternation and change, therefore for "becoming." Are the Greeks supposed to have grasped "being" as "becoming"? One finds in this thought a wealth of profundity. But perhaps it is only the thoughtlessness to which one flees in order to think neither about "being" nor about "becoming." And above all, the Greeks were far removed from this supposed profundity, despite Nietzsche, who, with the help of this empty opposition of being and becoming, has himself made grasping Greek thought impossible. Nevertheless, these concepts of *being* and *becoming* have a well delineated and essential meaning in Nietzsche's metaphysics. But neither Nietzsche's concepts of "becoming" and "being" nor Hegel's concepts of "becoming" and "being" may be thrown together with γένεσις as incipiently thought.

Γένεσις is spoken of, in that it is peculiar to what respectively presences. But this is *only* said *in addition*, not, however, with its own emphasis. For the fragment begins with ἐξ ὧν δὲ ἡ γένεσίς ἐστι τοῖς οὖσι, "whence emergence is for what respectively presences as a whole."

It does not talk about beings, also not about the being of beings, but it says from whence is emergence. But the fragment also does not intend to say this as if the "origin" of beings were constituted there in the sense of a primal ooze from which all things are produced. It speaks, rather, about the "origin" of being. Yet how does the passage say this? Where is the focal point of the first sentence?

Everything gathers itself together to say one thing: that from out of which emergence is peculiar to what respectively presences is the same as that back into which elusion γίνεσθαι, i.e., emerges. Once we have recognized what is supposed to be said, that the former, from out of which emergence presences, is just *the latter*, away into which evading presences, then there is no difficulty in finally reading this ταῦτα differently from the previous understanding of the text as ταὐτά. Only in this way does the wording first correspond to what the fragment intends to say.

The ταῦτα, "this" in the sense of ταὐτά, "the self-same" names that toward which all incipient thinking thinks, the self-sameness of the egress of emergence and the ingress of elusion. Yet, does not all of this remain indeterminate? What, then, is this self-same?

The fragment gives us the clear answer: κατὰ τὸ χρεών, emerging from the same and eluding into the same correspond to the compelling need. The compelling need is what all emergence and all elusion correspond to, when they emerge from the same and go into the same. Ταὐτά, the same, that is τὸ χρεών, the compelling need. Which need, we ask, which type of coercion holds sway here? Τὸ χρεών obviously does not mean just any kind of need, and also not coercion within a particular effective realm of beings. Τὸ χρεών is said directly from knowledge of the being of beings as a whole, yes, in knowledge of that from out of which the being of beings gets its egress and toward which it gets its return. We can never elucidate τὸ χρεών—the compelling need—through the citation of just any necessity, so that we think, for example, of the invariability of an effective law (e.g., the law of causality), or else substitute for the necessity named here that of "fate," as if with that the slightest thing could be clarified. Even if we could think such a thing, which is clearly not allowed here, the word "fate" is only another enigma and often only the now sincere and now insincere admission that we are at the limit of our knowledge.

To determine what τὸ χρεών means we must hold solely to the fragment of Anaximander. Moreover, from a unified understanding of this fragment we will first be in position to think in the direction the fragment indicates.

§23. Excursus: Insight into the τὸ χρεών with the help of another word from Anaximander

a) The threefold unity of enjoinment (ἀρχή)

Nevertheless, we will now interrupt the interpretation of the fragment for a moment, and follow the other, shorter, word that has been handed down to us from the thought of Anaximander:

(ἡ) ἀρχή τῶν ὄντων τὸ ἄπειρον.

"Enjoinment for the respectively present is the repelling of limits."

(Even more plainly handled: enjoinment as the repelling of the limit; this enjoining, however, as presencing of the disclosure of disclosedness as abiding.

The incipience of being resists duration.

But this very incipience withholds itself from what has been commenced.)

The Greek word ἀρχή is not yet used here in the later sense of *principium* and "principle." But the word itself is old and has for the Greeks a manifold meaning, which shall be pointed out soon.[12] Ἀρχή is that from

---

12. See Aristotle, *Physics* B. 1. [See also Martin Heidegger, "Vom Wesen und Begriff der Φύσις," *Wegmarken, Gesamtausgabe* 9 (Frankfurt, 1976), pp. 247ff. English translation: "On the Being and Conception of *Physis* in Aristotle's Physics B, 1," trans. Thomas J. Sheehan, *Man and World*, IX, 3 (April 1976): 219–270—Ed.]

whence something emerges. If we think ἀρχή solely in these terms, then the word means the beginning and the place of beginning for a process, a result. Then being a beginning involves being left behind in the course of the process. The beginning is there just to be abandoned and passed over. The beginning is always surpassed and left behind in the haste of going further. Were we to think of ἀρχή in such a way, as meaning "beginning," then we would give up all claim to the essential content at the outset.

To be sure, ἀρχή is that from which something emerges, but that from which something emerges retains, in what emerges and its emerging, the determination of motion and the determination of that toward which emergence is such. The ἀρχή is a way-making for the mode and compass of emergence. Way-making goes before and yet, as the incipient, remains behind by itself. Ἀρχή is not the beginning left behind in a progression. The ἀρχή releases emergence and what emerges, such that what is released is first retained in the ἀρχή as enjoinment. The ἀρχή is an enjoining egress. In this we perceive that from whence (ἐξ ὧν) there is emergence is the same as that back toward which evasion returns.

But not only this. The ἀρχή also disposes over what is between emerging and evading. This means, however, the ἀρχή enjoins precisely this between, which is no longer merely emergence but also no longer merely elusion: a transition. Transition is the actual emergence, its extremity, so to speak. The ἀρχή pervades transition. The ἀρχή is in itself an egress that everywhere prevails, that includes everything in its enjoinment and through this inclusion predetermines a domain and opens anything like a domain in the first place. Because egress and pervasiveness belong together in the essence of the ἀρχή, a third moment has determined itself, not as a result, but as an equally originary and essential moment: the domain-character of the ἀρχή, the measurable and the measured. With "measure" we do not think of numerical delimitation, but the opening domainness of the extension of enjoinment. The everywhere prevailing egress includes domainness within itself. Enjoinment would be perhaps the most likely and appropriate word for ἀρχή, if we grasp enjoinment in a threefold way:

1. Prevailing egress of emergence *and* elusion.
2. Pervading determination of the transition between emergence and elusion.
3. Holding open the opened domain of egressing pervasiveness.

Thus completely understood, ἀρχή contains the threefold unity of *egress, pervasiveness, and domain*.

These indications only want to give a hint for thinking the ἀρχή in the most fulfilled way. They want to avoid the arbitrariness of equating ἀρχή with a later philosophical concept of "principle." There predominates in the incipient not the poverty of any half- and one-sidedly grasped relation whatever, but an unmined wealth of relations. Despite this, we also cannot again mean that everything must therefore dissolve into indeterminacy. For throughout there stands here only what is singular, what is singular in reflecting and questioning.

b) Enjoinment (ἀρχή) is repelling (ἄπειρον)

The word of Anaximander says in what way the ἀρχή is: τὸ ἄπειρον—; one translates, that already means one "interprets," τὸ ἄπειρον with "the limitless," the "infinite." The translation is correct. However, it says nothing. Again, it is a matter of thinking within the radius of what is uniquely said here, of what enjoinment is to what presences, insofar as, and how it presences. Τὸ ἄπειρον, that which repels all limits, relates itself solely to the presencing of what presences, and it relates itself to this *as* ἀρχή, that means now in the threefold manner of egress, pervasiveness, and disclosure of domain. The ἀρχή pertains to being, and indeed so essentially that as ἀρχή it constitutes being itself.

But Anaximander talks about the ἀρχή τῶν ὄντων, the ἀρχή of those beings that presence. To be sure. However, we see from the first mentioned fragment that although something is said about what presences, something is *asked* about that from which and back toward which presencing presences. The ἀρχή pertains to being. Therefore the ἄπειρον cannot be thought as a being.

Nevertheless one interprets it thus and understands it as limitless being in the sense of a universal world-stuff. Accordingly, an undifferentiated world-soup would be imagined that is supposed to be not only without determination according to its own properties, but also without limits in its scope, and therefore inexhaustible at the same time. One forgets that we are supposed to *think* the saying of a thinker, indeed, a thinker in the inception, and not, for example, take note of the view of a failed "primitive" chemist. One does not consider that what is talked about is the enjoinment of being. Above all, however, one fails to reflect upon the fact that all Greek thinkers have experienced and grasped the being of beings as the presencing of those things that are present. It is not yet transparent that, and how, from this interpretation of being alone, what we call "Greek art," whether of words or sculpture, is also to be anticipated in its essence.

Τò ἄπειρον is the ἀρχή of being. Τò ἄπειρον is the repelling of limitation. It relates itself to being and only to being, and that means, in Greek, to the presencing of what presences.

How should we get to know this essential relationship better? If it were merely the content of a long disappeared doctrine we would have to give up all hope of knowing it. But in the fragment, being itself is said, and being remains for us overly near, surpassing all nearness of beings. Therefore, a hint of the familiar must still be preserved within what is strangest.

Enjoinment fits what presences into egress, pervasiveness, and domain. Enjoinment enjoins what we immediately call, and have called, beings into being. And only exclusively therein are they the beings that they are. Enjoinment is being itself, and enjoinment is ἄπειρον, the repelling of limit. Enjoinment is repelling.

This sounds strange, and at first hardly thinkable. But we must finally stay with this strangeness without any presuppositions. We already encounter something strange in this way of speaking. The first word that overtakes being contains a saying that is a refusal: ἄ-πειρον. One calls the ἀ, according to grammar, *privatum*; the "ἀ" expresses a "theft," a taking away, a lack and an absence. However, we mistrust grammar and stick to the matter.

The ἀρχή, the enjoinment, is itself distinguished by the α when it is the ἄ-πειρον. Enjoinment can obviously not, indeed can least of all, be something deficient. This, which is "without," the α, may be apprehended grammatically as the expression of "privation," but in substance and in essence it serves to properly determine, each time, the mode and means and possibility of the "away" and the "not." It could be that this "not" has in no way the character of something "negative." It could be that we—for a long time now—have understood the negative too negatively. How decisive the carefulness of thinking must be here may be confirmed even more by noting that in the inception of Western thought, not only the first word for being but also the determining word for truth has just this "privative" character. Truth is called ἀ-λήθεια, which, helplessly enough, we translate (without having provided the slightest clue) as *"unconcealment,"* in whose essential realm we must now think the thus-named "truth."

And when we think more inceptively into the inception, the question arises: Is there not an even more incipient relationship between the privative essence of being as ἄ-πειρον and the privative essence of truth as ἀ-λήθεια? Does not an essential unity of being and truth, still uninvestigated, announce itself here?

The α in ἄπειρον has the character of ἀρχή, and that means the character of enjoinment in respect to being and only in respect to being, to presencing. The α pertains to limits, limitation, and the removal of limits. But what does presencing have to do with limits? To what extent does an inner relationship to limit and limitation lie within presencing?

In presencing what presences determines itself as such. What presences comes into continuance through presence and is thus something that endures. The presencing of what endures has in itself a connection with and an inclination toward duration. And seen thus, duration obviously first attains its essence in steadfastness, in the persistence of a permanence made fast within itself. This lasting permanence would then first be what delimited the essence of presencing, and indeed such that this making fast in permanence would be the limitation that belongs to presencing. In essence, presencing would first be final through the finality of permanence.

However, the question remains whether and how duration and permanence correspond to the essence of presencing. This question can only be answered from what enjoins as the essence of presencing and as such enjoinment is called: ἀρχή τῶν ὄντων τὸ ἄπειρον. Enjoinment repels the limit for what presences. Being is presencing, but not necessarily duration in the sense of a hardening into permanence. However, does not all presencing fulfill itself precisely in the greatest possible duration? Is not a being more of a being the more steadfast and lasting it is? Does not the greatest possible securing of a being as a being lie in the greatest possible durability? Certainly—certainly, that is, in the sense of the *certainty* in which we contemporary ones think we know the being of beings. This certainty contains a truth about beings that reaches back even to the Greek thinkers: that permanence and duration, the ἀεί, lastingness, contains the highest distinction of the ὄν, of what presences. However, this incipient saying, ἀρχή τῶν ὄντων τὸ ἄπειρον, says something else. It only remains for us to fit ourselves to the saying, provided we want to hear its word and not our own opining.

c) The governance of being as ἀρχή and ἄπειρον in γένεσις and φθορά for the presencing of beings

Being is presencing, but not necessarily duration unto lasting permanence. For if permanence were precisely the non-essence of presencing, wouldn't permanence deprive presencing of something essential to it? To be sure. For γένεσις, presencing, does not mean mere presence, but emerging and opening up. Presencing is distinguished by γένεσις, emergence. Mere presence, in the sense of the present at hand, has already set a limit to presencing, emergence, and has thus given up presencing. Duration brings non-essence into presencing and takes from it the possibility of what belongs to presencing as emerging-forth and opening-up, that is, returning and eluding.

Emergence is not an abandonment of that from whence it has emerged. At most, what has emerged, a being, and only what has emerged, could be thought as if enjoinment had surrendered it. However, in truth that is impossible, because only emergence itself stands within enjoinment, which is the presencing enjoinment, but never what has emerged. On the contrary, emergence first actually sets the "from whence" into presencing, so the return into the "from whence" can only be the essential fulfillment of presencing.

What presences only presences in emerging and precisely not in the presence that has congealed into permanence. It belongs to the essence of presencing that its possible non-essence of hardening into something permanent is repelled in it. The enjoinment of presencing is a repelling of "limit," whereby limit means the closing off of presencing into a final presence, into the permanence of a mere presence. Accordingly, if presencing is to be preserved in its egressive essence, then emergence must emerge as a going back into the same. Γίνεσθαι must be in itself φθορά, evasion. Anaximander says, in fact: καὶ τὴν φθορὰν γίνεσθαι. Elusion also emerges, and emerges into the same. Γένεσις and φθορά, emergence and elusion, belong together. The unity of their belonging together is not the result of a subsequent piecing together, nor such that elusion merely follows after emergence. Emergence actually emerges as what eludes, it actually appears in this emergence when it is a transition. In transition emergence gathers itself in its essential fullness. In transition, as the emergence of the unity of emerging and evading, consists the respective presencing of what presences. However, transition does not involve itself in the limit of permanence. Thus transition preserves what is enjoined in enjoinment: τὸ ἄπειρον.

So the repelling of limit within presencing shows itself to be the enjoinment of the authentic being of beings. Ἀρχὴ τῶν ὄντων τὸ ἄπειρον. A being is not a being according to the extent to which it is something durable, but is something that presences, and indeed in the presencing that does not decay into mere presence. The steadfastness and lastingness of presencing are not decisive. The remaining of what remains also does not rest in mere continuance and its "proportions"; rather, the remaining of what remains is of another essence, provided that being nevertheless "remains" distinguished by a "remaining."

However, repelling the limit in the sense of holding back solidification into mere permanence would only be insufficiently grasped if we wanted to hear in it solely what accomplishes repelling. Repelling is at first, and that means in advance, relegation into presencing. Only insofar as repelling saves the essence of presencing beforehand ("preserves" it—in the sense of guarding), is repelling the limit (the ἄπειρον) also ἀρχή in the first sense: the egress of dispensation [*Fügung*] into essence. But when elusion above all remains included with the repelling of permanence in the essence of presencing, enjoinment is maintenance of the entire dispensing determination that lies enclosed within the essence of presencing. Repelling is the prevailing salvation of the essence of presencing, this, however, in the essential way of refusing the limit. Now, in which way does ἀρχή govern?

d) How does being, which is ἀρχή and ἄπειρον, let beings be?

The repelling that preserves its essence, τὸ ἄπειρον, is enjoinment in the threefold sense of egress, pervasiveness, and disclosure. This enjoinment as repelling is being itself. But how does being relate to beings? The question arises as to whether we are already allowed to pose the question this way here, where at first "only" being is supposed to be said.

We can only be assured of this one thing: enjoinment is not thought as something effective. Upon what is being supposed to "work"? Perhaps upon beings. But beings "are" indeed only what they are "in" enjoinment, indeed, as enjoinment. But enjoinment cannot cause and bring about beings, for everything effective is already a being, and enjoinment is being. Therefore, how does being let beings be? For somehow being is what presences, and both the names ἀρχή and ἄπειρον name exactly this. Thus there is also no place for the opinion that being exhausts itself in representing the most common and indifferent property of beings. But how does being, which now makes itself clear to us as ἀρχή and ἄπειρον, how does being let beings be?

Anaximander says: emergence and elusion emerge from and go away into the Same. The Same does not merely contain them both like a passive receptacle, but rather this emergence and evasion itself emerges according to the compelling need. It corresponds to the compelling need because the latter is the claim itself. It is itself the Same. This Same, enjoinment (ἀρχή), this Same, the ἄπειρον, is τὸ χρεών, need, what compels.

But where, in the previous reflection upon the ἀρχή τῶν ὄντων, do we apprehend something about need? Where else but in that which, as the fullness of essence, is called the ἀρχή, in the ἄπειρον? In repelling, when we think entirely within the essential fullness of what is to be said, there lies this: the self-defense of essence, and that means the salvation of the essence of presencing. Salvation of essence is preservation of the incipient. Such preservation of the essence is at the same time a self-defense against permanence as the non-essence of presencing. This essential salvation is the doubled preservation of essence.

Need does not mean misery and alienation, but compulsion in the sense of self-gathering in the inwardness of pure essence. Need does not mean lack and want, but the ineluctability of what is unique in its essence and so is relegated into uniqueness, and only into this, as something most its own. To need and necessity, thus grasped, belongs the warding off of duration and permanence, because this threatens essence as non-essence. But because this threat is nevertheless an essential one, warding off is not the self-defense of something being defeated, but of something gaining superiority. The compelling need τὸ χρεών contains the more fulfilled determination of the essence of the ἀρχή. That means: enjoinment as egress, pervasiveness, disclosure for emergence and elusion has the fundamental character of this compelling need. This need presences in the mode of the ἄπειρον, as a resistance that resists every limitation into final permanence. This compelling necessity, as enjoinment in the mode of resisting all limits, is that Same, from whence emerges all emergence and back into which eludes all elusion, wherein transition presences as the Same, and that means as the authentic presencing that does not succumb to permanence.

The reflection upon the shorter word of Anaximander, ἀρχὴ τῶν ὄντων τὸ ἄπειρον, can help us apprehend more clearly the word and concept τὸ χρεών, and therewith the naming of what is to be said in the first part of the fragment. For the Same, from whence comes emergence and back into which passes evasion, this Same is the compelling need. Τὸ χρεών does not mean a necessity added on somewhere next to and outside of the ἀρχή. This Same, one in its necessity, unique in its unity, and incipient in its uniqueness, is the *inception*. The inception is the essence of presencing as enjoinment of the presencing of what presences in each case: being itself. The fragment of Anaximander says being. The first sentence names being itself as the Same, in whose enjoinment each respectively presencing being is.

§24. The second sentence thinks being in correspondence with its essence as presencing, abiding, time

a) Being is overcoming the unfit

By comparison, the second sentence expressly says something only about beings: διδόναι γὰρ αὐτά. It is introduced with a γάρ, "namely," "for." We have already noted that the meaning is not immediately univocal. After a clarification of the first, the relation between both sentences can now be more precisely thought out. But here it is also advisable to first think out the main features of the second sentence, and thus to grasp again what bears importance and weight.

It is said of things respectively presencing that they always give what is fitting of themselves and give acknowledgment to one another, all of this, however, τῆς ἀδικίας. The genitive expresses that what respectively presences, and indeed as itself, i.e., in its respective presencing, stands in relation to ἀδικία, to the unfit. How should we understand this?

The unfit belongs to what respectively presences. This means: what does not fit itself into enjoinment. However, insofar as what presences presences, it stands in enjoinment and satisfies enjoinment. In each case what presences is what presences from itself as a being, ὄντα αὐτά. Certainly—but precisely the fact that a being is each time a being from itself means this: that being, i.e., presencing, consists in itself of endurance unto permanence. To the essence of presencing, taken for itself, belongs this persistence: that presencing presences, i.e., finds its finality in an endurance and its completion in such an end (limit). In the presencing of what presences (ὄντα αὐτά) lies duration as persisting in permanence. In this word we must not merely think the continuance and final lastingness of presencing, but, at the same time and above all, the "persistence," the final insistence upon the evermore (the ἀεί).

Thus conceived, however, permanence is contrary to the egressively enjoined essence of being, contrary to the ἀρχή, contrary to the ἄπειρον, the repelling of limit. But what presences essentially and yet contrary to the essence is the *non-essence*. What solidifies the enjoined upon itself, unto permanence and contrary to enjoinment, is the *unfit*, ἀδικία. This does not come to what presences from just anywhere, but is included in the essence of presencing and belongs to the necessity of being. This is, in itself, as the repelling of limit, already related to limitation unto permanence and thus to the unfit as a presencing possibility (inclination). (The "privative" character of the unfit thus attests simultaneously, as the counter-essence, to the essence of being, which has a "privative" character in the incipient sense of enjoinment itself: τὸ ἄπειρον.)

To the extent that what respectively presences corresponds to the essence of presencing, it does not consist in and solidify into duration unto permanence. Presencing is emergence as transition. What presences in this way gives what is fit, δίκην. It fits itself into enjoinment. That means to say: presencing is the transition of emergence into elusion. However, beings themselves give what is fit to being, and as beings of such an essence, they also allow each respective being to be what it is of itself. Giving what is fit to being, every being mutually acknowledges every other. Each thus allows the other its appropriate regard (καὶ τίσιν ἀλλή-λοις). The full essential relation of what respectively presences to the unfit determines itself only through this duality in which the various moments belong together in themselves (διδόναι δίκην καὶ τίσιν ἀλλή-λοις). Giving what is fit and granting mutual acknowledgment—that is in itself overcoming [*Verwindung*] the unfit. We do not say subduing [*Überwindung*] because that could mean the unfit would be eliminated. Indeed, the unfit belongs to the essence of presencing as non-essence. Permanence is not subdued in the sense of a complete dissolution, i.e., the revocation of its essential possibility. On the contrary: the essential tendency toward the unfit presences, but is overcome. What presences does not let itself become involved in the unfit, so far as it is something that presences. Overcoming the unfit belongs to the essence of what respectively presences as such, for as such it fits itself into transition. This self-fitting, however, is an according with the claim that lies in every transitoriness.

Transition is always presencing in which emergence and evasion presence above all. Transition thus contains in itself that Same, whence coming to be and whither passing away presence, indeed, transition is the pure emerging of that Same. This Same is being itself.

b) The connection between being and time

In transition, i.e., when what presences overcomes the unfit and does not persist unto permanence, what presences fits itself in each case to *its own* presencing, and accommodates itself to this. In this way it fulfills the "when" and "how long" that are allotted to each respective being. In overcoming the unfit, what presences corresponds to the allotment of temporalizing by time. And conversely, this correspondence with "time" is nothing other than overcoming the unfit.

What does "time" (χρόνος) mean here, and why does the fragment say something about the being of time?

The modern habit of thinking time together with "space" (already prefigured in the beginning of metaphysics with Aristotle) leads us astray. For according to this way of thinking time is considered solely in terms of its extension, and this as a counting up of fleeting now-points. Thought in modern terms, time is a parameter, like space, a standard scale according to which something is measured and estimated. Space and time are essentially related to "calculation."

However, in Greek χρόνος means what corresponds to τόπος, to the place where each respective being belongs. Χρόνος is the always favorable and granted time as distinguished from the untimely. Τάξις never means a serial ordering of now-points one after the other, but the allotment-character that lies within time itself as what is always the proper [*schicklich*], sending [*schickenden*], granting, and ordaining time. We do not apprehend "time" when we say "Time is . . . ." We are closer to apprehending it when we say "It is time." That always means it is time that this happens, this comes, this goes. What we thus address as time is in itself the kind of thing that directs and allots. Time is the allotment of presencing for what presences in each case. Time is the expansion of the respectively enjoined abiding [*Weile*], according to which what presences is always something *momentary* [*jeweiliges*]. In overcoming the unfit of itself, the momentarily presencing αὐτά corresponds to the enjoined abiding of transition. By giving what is fit to enjoinment, and by each one mutually acknowledging the other, each respective presencing corresponds to the allotment of abiding. That beings are in the respective correspondence of their "being" to "time" means nothing other than: *Being itself is lingering, presencing.*

What remains unsaid is that being, so presencing, has the enjoinment of its essence in time. Why the fragment says something about the being of time has its (unspoken) ground in the fact that being itself is "experienced" as presencing, and this is "experienced" as the transition of emergence into elusion. Presencing is abiding, and its non-essence lies in the lingering that would like to persist unto a final duration. The essence of being repels this limit. In abiding, which is always essentially only *an* abiding, being extricates itself from the unfit, and, through elusion, saves that One and Same as what solely enjoins, which is egress and pervasiveness and disclosure for every being.

§25. The relation of both sentences to one another: The fragment as the incipient saying of being

In what relation, then, stand the first and second sentences of the fragment?

The *first* sentence says that emergence and elusion, which in their unity make up the essence of being, emerge from the Same. Elusion also "emerges." This Same is the inception of being, is being as the inception.

The *second* sentence speaks of beings (αὐτά τὰ ὄντα), and it says how a being is as a being. The second sentence simply names being and names it as overcoming the unfit. The second sentence in no way gives a grounding for the first. The fragment does not want to explain emergence from the Same and elusion into the Same by characterizing beings as determined by the unfit. Rather, the reverse is the case. Being is overcoming the unfit, that means not insisting upon endurance, because transition belongs to the essence of being.

The *second* sentence puts into words the experiencing of being. Transition reveals itself to this experiencing as pure, self-gathered emergence. Thinking receives from such experiencing the directive in respect to which the essence of being and the inception of this essence is to be thought. And this is said by the *first* sentence. 'That is' [γὰρ], because beings presence in their being according to the allotment of the proper time, the essence of being must be enclosed within presencing. Such is the case insofar as presencing has the character of abiding, which determines itself from transition and as transition.

Abiding is a lingering for its time, a lingering that "only" allows itself a while. But this 'only' does not mean a restriction; rather, it says the purity of the inwardness of the essence of being: the elusive egress as transition. Nevertheless, transition presences only such that the Same enjoins emergence and elusion, which enjoinment is compelling need.

The first sentence names the inception of the essence of what is named by the second: being. It says something about being like the second, but the first says something about being in a different way. Both sentences name a correspondence (κατὰ . . .). The second thinks being in correspondence with its essence, i.e., to presencing, i.e., to abiding, i.e., to "time." The first sentence thinks the thus experienced essence in correspondence to its "inception," i.e., to enjoinment (ἀρχή), which, as the Same, pervades the essential features of presencing (emergence and elusion in their unity) in expanding for them their domain in which each being is momentary so far as it lingers for *its* while.

In every word the fragment speaks of being and only of being, even where it actually names beings (τοῖς οὖσι), (αὐτά). *The fragment says the enjoinment of being and being as enjoinment. Enjoinment, however, is the inception. The fragment is the incipient saying of being.*

Knowing this is the first condition for remembrance into the inception. But this one thing remains essential: incipiently, being "is" enjoinment, which repels all limits in the sense of duration. In such repelling, enjoinment saves itself back *into* itself, in the Same that is itself. Only thus is the inception the inception, which can only presence in being incipient. However, as a returning into itself, the inception is the most concealed. All of this first reveals itself when thinking is incipient once again.

(Ταὐτά as from whence emergence and whither elusion. But what is the whither of emergence and the away from of elusion? Presencing as transition. The unconcealing concealing (ἀλήθεια).

To this extent the unsaid ἀλήθεια and ταὐτά, which means ἄπειρον, are, yet again and even more incipiently, the Same.)

EDITOR'S EPILOGUE

Martin Heidegger held a one-hour weekly lecture course entitled "Grundbegriffe" in the winter semester of 1941 at Freiburg University.

Heidegger understands "Grundbegriffe" literally, i.e., as "Grounds," concepts that ground everything, that alone give all grounds and make a claim upon man in his essence. Since the inception of Western thought, man has been affected by being in his essence, admitted into being as having his true abode there. However, being 'comports' itself in a twofold way: it is the origin of all beings in withholding itself. Thus it could happen in the course of the history of metaphysics that beings became more and more the preeminent theme of thinking. Since modern times especially, thinking has increasingly solidified into a calculation of the useful. But in order to think the ground, which means tearing being away from its forgottenness and thinking against everyday "thinking," remembrance into the inception is necessary. For Heidegger, returning into the inception of thinking means therefore: considering the saying of being and the saying about being by the inceptive thinkers. In reflecting upon the saying μελέτα τὸ πᾶν, Heidegger elucidates the essential difference between being and beings as *the* difference into which man is admitted. Guidewords about being allow its incomprehensibility for logical thought to become visible in such a way that a first given determination immediately runs into a second, opposite determination. But Heidegger does not want to understand this process as dialectical.

What we have called "Part Two" gives a detailed interpretation of two fragments by Anaximander. The 1946 essay entitled "The Anaximander Fragment," previously published in *Holzwege*, takes up individual thoughts from this interpretation once again; but each of them is a completely independent elaboration.

A transcription carried out by Fritz Heidegger in May 1944 served as the basis for this edition. Handwritten marginalia by Martin Heidegger clearly indicate his corrections and revisions of the text. The original handwritten manuscript was lent out by Martin Heidegger and was never returned.

The text of the lectures runs continuously and comprises 75 typewritten pages. In addition, there are 29 pages of "Recapitulations," composed separately and provided with their own pagination. The content of these "Recapitulations" extends as far as the interpretation of the Anaximander fragment (Part Two). The "Recapitulations" were incorporated into the main text here, as was done in volume 55, in compliance with Martin Heidegger's instructions.

Since the typewritten materials contain no divisions, the articulation into parts, sections, and paragraphs, as well as the formulations of their titles, was provided by the editor. The wording of the table of contents closely follows what Heidegger set forth. Its detail gives an overview of each new step in Heidegger's thinking at the outset.

For their experienced assistance in the preparation of this volume, I would like to thank very sincerely Professor Fr.-W. v. Herrmann for his inexhaustible willingness to answer many technical questions and Professor W. Biemel and Dr. H. Heidegger for their advice and expert judgment in all editorial matters. I also owe thanks to Eva-Maria Hollenkamp for her assistance in reviewing the pageproofs.

PETRA JAEGER

GLOSSARY

to abide	*weilen*
abiding	*die Weile*
to anticipate	*ahnen*
anticipation	*die Ahnung*
becoming	*das Werden*
beginning	*der Beginn*
being	*das Sein*
beings	*das Seiende*
coming to be	*das Entstehen*
continuance	*der Bestand*
disclosedness	*die Entborgenheit*
disclosure	*die Entbergung*
dispensation	*die Fügung*
to dispense, to fit	*fügen*
domain	*der Bereich*
duration, endurance	*die Beständigung*
egress	*der Ausgang*
elusion	*die Entgängnis*
emergence	*der Hervorgang*
to enjoin, to fit	*verfügen*
enjoinment	*die Verfügung*
essence	*das Wesen*
evading, evasion	*das Entgehen*
the fit	*der Fug*
historical	*geschichtliche*
historiological	*historische*
historiology	*die Historie*
history	*die Geschichte*
inception	*Der Anfang*
incipient	*anfänglich*
ingress	*der Eingang*
limit	*der Grenze*
need	*die Not*
non-essence	*das Unwesen*
origin	*der Ursprung*
originary	*ursprünglich*

to overcome	*verwinden*
overcoming	*die Verwindung*
passing away	*das Vergehen*
permanence	*die Beständigkeit*
persistence	*das Bestehen*
to pervade	*durchwalten*
pervasiveness	*die Durchwaltung*
(mere) presence	*die Anwesenheit*
presence, presencing (beings)	*die Anwesung*
presence, presencing (essence)	*die Wesung*
presencing (beings)	*das Anwesen*
presencing (essence)	*wesen*
to prevail	*vor(aus)walten*
repelling	*die Verwehrung*
steadfastness	*die Ständigkeit*
to subdue	*überwinden*
transition	*der Übergang*
the unfit	*der Unfug*
unique	*einzig*
what endures, is durable	*das Beständige*